A GOLDEN TREASURY OF IRISH POETRY

A GOLDEN TREASURY OF IRISH POETRY

A.D. 600 to 1200

Edited and with translations by
David Greene and Frank O'Connor

BRANDON

This paperback edition published in 1990 by
Brandon Ireland & UK Ltd
Dingle, Co. Kerry

Original edition published in 1967 by Macmillan

© Introduction, commentaries and translations
David Greene and Frank O'Connor 1967

British Library Cataloguing in Publication Data
A Golden treasury of Irish poetry, A.D. 600 to A.D. 1200.
 1. Poetry in Irish, to 1700 – Anthologies
 I. Greene, David II. O'Connor, Frank, *1903-1966*
 891.621108

ISBN 0-86322-113-0

Cover design by The Graphiconies
Printed by The Guernsey Press Co. Ltd,
Guernsey, Channel Islands

TO

HILARY AND HARRIET

WHOSE TACTFUL ABSENCES FROM

THE SCENE ALONE MADE THIS

BOOK POSSIBLE

CONTENTS

LIST OF ABBREVIATIONS	*page*	ix
AN INTRODUCTION		1
1 Hymn to St. Colum Cille		19
2 Jesus and the Sparrows		23
3 Jesus at School		25
4 Breastplate Number One		27
5 Breastplate Number Two		33
6 The Nativity		36
7 The Crucifixion		40
8 The Two Worlds		44
9 The Nun of Beare		48
10 Invocation to the Martyrs		56
11 The Downfall of Heathendom		61
12 To St. Brigit		67
13 Líadan		72
14 The Ex-Poet		75
15 Ordeal by Cohabitation		77
16 Créd's Lament		78
17 The Scholar and his Cat		81
18 Writing Out-of-doors		84
19 The Dead Lover		86
20 Rónán's Lament		93
21 Winter		98
22 The Pity of Nature — I		100
23 Ita and the Infant Jesus		102
24 Triads		104
25 Dramatis Personae		107
26 Men and Women — I		111

CONTENTS

27	Paradise Revised	115
28	Prayer for a Long Life	123
29	The Tempest	126
30	The Only Jealousy of Emer	130
31	Winter	134
32	Summer	137
33	The Four Seasons	140
34	A Prayer for Recollection	144
35	The Hermitage	148
36	The Pilgrim	151
37	Fellow Feeling	154
38	Eve	157
39	The Scribe	159
40	Faith	161
41	Hymn to St. Michael	165
42	Mael Ísu finds his Psalter again	167
43	Grace before Death	171
44	The Lament for Fer Diad	174
45	The Song of the Heads	176
46	The Pity of Nature — II	179
47	Colum Cille in Exile	181
48	Lullaby of Adventurous Love	184
49	A Winter Night	189
50	Massacre of the Innocents	191
51	The Last Call-up	195
52	Medieval Diary	200
53	Men and Women — II	202
54	Storm and Birdsong	205
INDEX OF TITLES		209
INDEX OF NAMES		211

LIST OF ABBREVIATIONS

AU	*Annals of Ulster* (W. M. Hennessey and B. MacCarthy, eds.; Dublin, (vol. II) 1893, (vol. III) 1895).
Auraicept	*Auraicept na nÉces* (George Calder, ed.; Edinburgh, 1917).
BB	Book of Ballymote.
Bruchstücke	*Bruchstücke der älteren Lyrik Irlands* (Kuno Meyer; Berlin 1919).
Dictionary	*Dictionary of the Irish Language* (Royal Irish Academy; in course of publication).
EIL	*Early Irish Lyrics* (Gerard Murphy, ed.; London, 1956).
Félire Óengusso	*Félire Óengusso Céli Dé* (W. Stokes, ed.; for the Henry Bradshaw Society, 1905).
FM	*Annals of the Four Masters* (J. O'Donovan, ed.; Dublin, 1851).
GJ	*Gaelic Journal.*
IT	*Irische Texte* (W. Stokes and E. Windisch; Leipzig, 1880–1909).
ISP	*An Introduction to Irish Syllabic Poetry of the Period 1200–1600* (Eleanor Knott; Cork, 1924).
ITS	Irish Texts Society.

LB	Leabhar Breac.
LL	Book of Leinster.
LU	Lebor na hUidre (Book of the Dun Cow) (printed edition cited is that of R. I. Best and O. Bergin; Dublin, 1929).
NLI	National Library of Ireland.
OIr.	Old Irish.
PRIA	*Proceedings of the Royal Irish Academy.*
RC	*Revue celtique.*
Thes.	*Thesaurus Palaeohibernicus* (W. Stokes and J. Strachan, eds.; Cambridge, 1901).
ZCP	*Zeitschrift für celtische Philologie.*

AN INTRODUCTION

I

There are four distinct periods of poetry in Irish: from the sixth to the twelfth century, from the twelfth to the sixteenth, from the sixteenth to the decline of Irish as a written language at the beginning of the nineteenth, and the revival period from the end of the nineteenth to the present day. These periods correspond fairly close with linguistic phases: the first with Old and Middle Irish, the second with Classical Modern Irish, and the third and fourth with Modern Irish proper. In each period the status and training of the poet are different. In the first he is a product of the fusion of the old learning with that of the monastic schools and is usually a cleric himself; in the second he belongs to the lay and hereditary professional class usually, though wrongly, called the bardic; in the third he is little more than a peasant who has preserved some fragments of the older tradition, meeting with his colleagues at an inn to hold a poetic court; in the fourth he is, like so many elsewhere, merely a part-time poet. Only during the first of these periods was Ireland an independent country, and only then did the Irish have an indigenous prose literature; the poetry of this period is easily the most important of the four, and in our opinion the most important branch of medieval poetry. Unfortunately the manuscript tradition is very bad indeed; for the greater part of our period we depend on late copies of the poems, botched by antiquarians and modernized by scribes. Perhaps the outstanding example is the fact that the first poem we print here, which we ascribe to the seventh century, exists only in a seventeenth-century manuscript, though here the text is in fact fairly well preserved. To present an early Irish poem to the general reader demands editing and emending, and this we have done; when verses, or whole poems, were unintelligible to us, we have simply left them out.

The ingredients of Irish literature when it first appears are traditional — genealogy, history, and law; it has much more in common with the Pentateuch than with the urbanized literatures of Greece and Rome. Its original custodians were the *filid*, or 'seers', who passed on the tradition, orally, in the form of alliterative verse. The earliest composition to which we can attach a date is an elegy on St. Colum Cille composed at the time of his death in 597 by Dallán Forgaill; it is mainly in alliterative chant. For the actual transmission of information there was also a number of metres of a more practical kind; notably a seven-syllable line with a caesura after the fourth syllable. This continued to be used even after the early period; a beautiful Middle Irish pastiche will be found in the four poems on the seasons. These poems close with the word that begins them; two words in each line alliterate, and alliterate again with the first stressed word of the next line. The poetic phrase, which may be of any length, is terminated by a line of five syllables. Thus:

> *The heavy ground is filled with fruit,*
> *And by the fort, hard from their height,*
> *Hazelnuts break and fall.*

The metrical system was based on mnemonic patterns; it gave the reciter a valuable check on the accuracy of his performance, and is of considerable help to the modern editor in restoring corrupt texts.

In the second half of the sixth century rhyme began to

find its way into the metres. We see this process at work in a few fragments by Colmán mac Lénini, who died in the year 604 as Abbot of Cloyne in County Cork. St. Colmán began his life as a professional poet, and the seven fragments of his verse that have been collected by Rudolf Thurneysen are both religious and secular; except from the historical point of view they are of no great interest, and a single fragment will serve as an example of his work. It is from a poem in praise of the sword given him as a fee by a prince called Domnall who later became King of Tara:

> Luin oc elaib,
>   ungi oc dírnaib,
> drecha ban n-aithech
>   oc ródaib rígnaib;
> ríg oc Domnall,
>   dord oc aidbse
> adand oc caindil,
>   calg oc mo chailgse.[1]

Blackbirds compared with swans, ounces with hundredweights, peasant women's faces with great queens; kings compared with Domnall, yodelling with a choir, a spark compared with a candle, is every sword compared with my sword.

This derives from an oral tradition, with chain alliteration — the last word of each line alliterating with the first word in the next. It also contains rhyme, of the kind Irish used from this period up to the end of the Classical Modern period. Since in Irish, as in English, there are few perfect rhymes for words of more than one syllable, it is permitted to rhyme consonants that are similar phonetically, just as Shakespeare does when he rhymes 'token' with 'open'. We

[1] ZCP, xix, 198.

have already arrived at the kind of metre in which nearly all the poems we deal with are written; its characteristics are alliteration, fixed number of syllables in a line, and rhyme of the Irish kind. Chain alliteration, however, becomes less and less common in the later part of our period.

The first poem we print belongs to the early type; it is part of a hymn to St. Colum Cille, written less than a century after his death. There is the same sort of rhyming system that we find in Colmán's verses, but there the similarity ends, for the author of the Columban hymn — a professional poet like Colmán — has also mastered the secret of Virgilian rhetoric, and the third and fourth lines are something entirely new in Irish poetry and indicate that it has come of age.

*Sét fri úathu úair no tías
ní cen toísech, táthum nert.*

But this poem is exceptional — it would be exceptional in any language. The literary work of the early monastic schools is better represented in the eighth-century Biblical poems discovered and edited by Professor James Carney. Neither of the authors whose work he has printed was a professional poet in the manner of St. Colmán or the seventh-century hymn-writer. Their aim was instruction and edification, and the literary beauty which they so often achieved might almost be described as accidental. The author of the versified 'Apocryphal Gospel of St. Thomas', for example, was unaware of the stupidity of the text on which he was working, but he wrote with the freshness and charm we associate with the beginning of literature in any country. His verse falls naturally into the rhythms of the early English carols.

When he was only five years old
  Jesus, son of God,
Made twelve little waterholes
  In the wet mud.

Then he made twelve little birds —
  Passeres as they say;
He made them on the Sabbath
  Faultlessly of clay.

A certain Jew denounced him
  For what he had done,
And by the hand to Joseph
  He took God's only son.

'Correct your son, Joseph,
  For on the Sabbath day
He made graven images
  From the wet clay.'

Jesus clapped his hands;
  His voice was clear and bright;
Before their eyes, a marvel,
  The little birds took flight.

And then the voice of Jesus
  Was heard to proclaim:
'To show you know who made you
  Go back whence you came!'

Another Jew reported
  Without a word of lie
That far in the distance
  He heard the birds cry.

The inspiration of the early Irish Church had been the Bible and the Psalms. We see this in the contemporary description of the Irish monks by Bede, who, while admiring their sanctity, deplored their intellectual limitations. By the beginning of the eighth century the monasteries had changed considerably. The greater ones, such as Armagh and Clonmacnois, had begun to turn into towns, and the abbots who ruled them were already beginning to be described as *principes*. They were wealthy, worldly, scholarly men who lived in comfortable houses, with libraries and wine cellars, and their sons and daughters, who would also find careers in the Church, studied Irish as well as Latin. A vast secular literature had grown up within the monasteries, based on the traditional material of the professional poets, whose version of history was exceedingly popular with the monks; in the twelfth-century satire 'The Vision of Mac Con Glinne' there is a delightful description of an abbot, his Wellington boots stuffed with manuscripts — in one 'The Cattle Raid of Cooley' and 'The Destruction of Dá Derga's Hostel' and in the other 'The Wooing of Étaín' and 'The Wooing of Emer'. This developed far beyond the preservation of the tradition; by the end of the Old Irish period we begin to find stories that, although told about historical personages, conflict completely with the evidence available in the annals and genealogies. Stories are now being told for their own sake, and creative literature appears.

This imaginative literature had a strange ecclesiastical counterpart — Church history written in the manner of the old sagas. The saints — heroes of these pseudo-sagas — were conceded conceptions, births, and childhood adventures far more extraordinary than those of Cú Chulainn and his kind, and were recorded as destroying more enemies with their prayers and curses than the true saga heroes destroyed with their swords. At its crudest the pseudo-saga deals with the life of a saint who is obstructed or insulted by a king, and brings the king to ruin and death by his miracles. In one story Aed mac Ainmire, King of Tara, asks his half-brother, the Abbot of Glendalough, to swear in the heathen way by his testicles, and the abbot prophesies that a wolf will soon eat the king's own testicles, which it does. In another story an Ulster king called Suibne quarrels with a saint named Rónán, is driven mad, and dies a horrible death.

The new 'literary' saga, whether lay or ecclesiastical, is of considerable interest to us, for much good verse appears in it. Although prose — and usually excellent prose — is the true medium of the saga proper, it was customary to use heightened language at dramatic moments — often for a dialogue between two characters — and in the later sagas this heightened language takes the form of verse. A well-known example is Cú Chulainn's lament over Fer Diad; others are the poems which terminate 'Fingal Rónáin', and the fine nature poetry put into the mouth of Suibne in the story mentioned above. Sometimes it is difficult to decide whether the prose and poetry are really by the same hand; the situation is even worse when the prose has been lost, or is reduced to a cryptic and garbled introduction to the poem. This is precisely our situation with some of the finest poems in our collection, which seem to derive from a group of pseudo-sagas, most of which is lost, dealing with St. Cummíne the Tall, a Kerryman; his friend Guaire, King of Aidne, whose capital was Gort in County Galway; Guaire's brother, Mongán, a hermit monk; his daughter Créd and her West Limerick lover, Dínertach; his friend Mac Dá Cerda, a Holy Fool; Líadan, the Cork poetess, and her poet lover from Connacht, Cuirithir; and last, and most important, the Nun of Beare, subject of the greatest of Irish poems.

Some of these characters are probably historical. Cummíne

certainly did write the penitential ascribed to him, but since he turns up in Munster legends as the child of an incestuous union it would seem that he was already turning into folk-lore. Líadan may be the St. Líadan who gave her name to a County Limerick church. Guaire, too, may be historical; his brother is probably a fiction, and his daughter was originally probably intended to represent his wife.

We have had to omit 'King and Hermit', the beautiful poem in which Mongán expounds to Guaire the charms of the hermit's life, because the text is simply too bad to extract a version that would at the same time satisfy ourselves and interest the general reader whom we have in mind. But we have printed Créd's lament for the death of Dínertach; verses from the story of Líadan and Cuirithir in which St. Cummíne intervenes disastrously in a love affair between two poets, and 'The Nun of Beare', in which he appears as spiritual director of an ex-mistress of the kings of Munster.

What makes these pseudo-sagas so remarkable is that the conflict between the secular and the religious approach is treated with such extraordinary gravity and maturity. Guaire, the king, does not meet with a horrible end because of some disagreement with St. Cummíne, though in the matter of maturity readers may consult another pseudo-saga from Mayo, 'The Life of Cellach', in which he appears as the villain; Cuirithir does not go to Hell because he will not accept the rude sexual discipline of Clonfert, and even the Nun of Beare is politely permitted her great song in praise of worldly joy.

It may be that this maturity can be explained in terms of a common authorship; certainly there is a common tradition of authorship. 'Créd' is clearly intended to be spoken by a married woman, for no unmarried girl in an Irish story would describe herself as being 'in the instability of age', nor would she say of her father, 'I have every good with Guaire, the King of cold Aidne'. Possibly it is a lyric from a romance which described the moral problem of a passionate woman married to a kind and generous husband. Two of the twenty-four lines echo lines from 'The Nun of Beare': 'my mind seeks to go' and 'my wantonness has begun to deceive me'. The curious and beautiful lines 'sweeter than all songs was his speech, except for holy adoration of the King of Heaven' are also reminiscent of lines in 'Líadan and Cuirithir': 'It would be madness not to do his pleasure if it were not for fear of the King of Heaven'. More than anything else in Irish these lines define precisely the conflict between the saga and the pseudo-saga, the secular and religious, but they define it in human terms.

'The Nun of Beare' is the most difficult text we have had to tackle, and we are far from satisfied with the result. At one point we attempted a complete textual rearrangement, and abandoned it only because it was impossible to discover what the original prose context of the pseudo-saga was. The first verse requires a setting by the sea with the Nun old and poor, but the third, fourth, and fifth show her in a midland plain riding in a chariot and speaking to a group of young men whom we have not met before and shall not meet again, and whom she describes as useless lovers. Some of the verses are clearly spoken by a man, presumably St. Cummíne, mentioned in the brief prose introduction as having consecrated the Nun. That a dotty eleventh-century editor has been at work, obliterating the prose framework and making a single poem out of what in effect were probably half a dozen poems, is suggested by the first verse —

> *Ebbtide is all my grief,*
>   *Old age has sucked my blood,*
> *But, though I get no relief,*
>   *Merrily returns its flood.*

Clearly, this verse has been misplaced to provide a first word that can be echoed as the last, and its real place is immediately before the verse that runs:

> *Happy island of the main,*
> *To you the tide returns again,*
> *Though to me it comes no more*
> *Over the deserted shore.*

II

About the year 800, on the eve of the first Viking raids, a fine poet, Óengus of Clonenagh, celebrated the triumph of the Irish Church in verses that deserve to be classical.

> *Old haunts of the heathen*
>   *Filled from ancient days*
> *Are but deserts now*
>   *Where no pilgrim prays.*
>
> *Little places taken*
>   *First by twos and threes*
> *Are like Rome reborn,*
>   *Peopled sanctuaries.*
>
> *Heathendom has gone down*
>   *Though it spread everywhere;*
> *God the Father's kingdom*
>   *Fills heaven and earth and air.*

Óengus believed that he was writing about a state of affairs that would endure for ever, but within a few years all the great monasteries, which were built of timber and wattle and daub, were in ashes. It was fully a hundred years before they could be rebuilt; and then the work was usually carried out in stone — stone churches, towers, and crosses. At the same time there was a vast increase in the influence of the professional poets with their antiquarian lore. Óengus himself was a professional poet, but, like his predecessor Bláthmacc, he was interested primarily in edification. His immediate successor, another Leinsterman, who was Bishop of Kildare, Orthanach, had no such prejudice. In a fine poem on Kildare he attempted, like Óengus, to contrast the glory of the Christian settlement with the deserted state of the old pagan forts, but got completely lost in the process because the Leinster capital, Alenn, appealed far more to him than Kildare itself.

Though this reversion to antiquarianism began before the invasions, its strength must be due to a certain decline in the monastic schools themselves, which were now being attacked by Irishmen as well as Norsemen and offered only a precarious shelter for humanists. We gather as much from a bitter little fragment of a poem on the plundering of Clonmacnois, the metre of which is probably eleventh century.

> '*Whence are you, learning's son?*'
> '*From Clonmacnois I come;*
> *My course of studies done,*
>   *I am off to Swords again.*'
> '*How are things shaping there?*'
> '*Oh, things are keeping fair;*
> *Foxes round churchyards bare*
>   *Gnawing the guts of men.*'

Even so, Kildare itself seems to have managed to keep up a considerable classical school, for a group of Leinster scholars seems to have passed through Wales to the Continent during Orthanach's own lifetime, one of whom was Sedulius of Liège. During the reign of Charlemagne, Europe ceased to ask for missionaries from Ireland and asked instead for schoolmasters, and this is marked in Irish literature by a switch in significance from the Bible to the classics. One of those travelling scholars picked up a pet cat called Pangur in Wales, and Pangur became the subject of one of the most beautiful of medieval lyrics, the author of which certainly knew his Horace.

In spite of the often demented antiquarianism, the old spirit of the literature was very much alive and renewing itself in all sorts of odd ways. In a poem like 'The Dead Lover' the poet's task was to list the treasures of a dead mercenary chieftain, but in doing so he also produced one of the most beautiful poems in any language. The attention that professional poets were devoting to metrical experiment is another positive aspect of the literary scholarship that would eventually drag them down. We have three handbooks of prosody still unedited; one from the ninth, another from the tenth, and a third from the late eleventh century, and though the metres become progressively more complicated, new metres like that of the poem on the plundering of Clonmacnois were being introduced from Latin.

Besides, there seems to have been a revival of interest in the old alliterative metres, and in two scenes in 'Bricriu's Feast' and 'The Sick-bed of Cú Chulainn' some poet tried to revive the old dramatic form of story-telling as we find it in the earliest strata of the sagas. Some other metrist, as skilful as Robert Bridges, wrote a group of poems on the seasons as though to show how the alliterative metres could be used in a contemporary way.

> *Fall is no man's travelling time;*
> *Tasks are heavy; husbandmen*
> *Need horses as the light grows less;*
> *Lightly their young drop from the deer,*
> *Dandled in the faded fern;*
> *Fiercely the stag stalks from the hill,*
> *Hearing the herd in clamorous call.*
> *Cobbled the mast in windless woods;*
> *Weary the corn upon its canes,*
>   *Colouring the brown earth.*
> *Endless the thorns that foul the fence*
> *That frames the hollow of some house;*
> *The heavy ground is filled with fruit,*
> *And by the fort, hard from their height,*
>   *Hazelnuts break and fall.*

As one sees from this, nature poetry was very much alive, and nature poetry is the most extraordinary feature of early Irish literature and by far the hardest to explain. That it was of native origin we are compelled to believe if we accept Gerard Murphy's theory that it originated with the hermits of the sixth and seventh centuries, or Kenneth Jackson's that it originated in pagan seasonal songs. Either is hard to justify, because nature poetry disappeared completely in the twelfth century, and it is difficult to see how this could happen to a native form.

A number of the poems and fragments are demonstrably of a late date. One of the best known is a fragment from a poem about the sea in flood. 'See away to the north-east, the majestic whale-haunted sea; the abode of seals, playful and splendid, is in full flood.' The verse form is in eight lines, and the eight-line verse does not come into Irish until about the eleventh century. Besides, though the syllables have been counted, the poem itself is stressed. Except for the unstressed syllable at the beginning of the third and seventh lines, the metre is identical with that of a twelfth-century French love song.

> *Le jalous*
> *Envious*
> *De cor rous*
> *Morra;*
> *Et li dous*
> *Savourous*
> *Amourous*
> *M'aura.*

Unless we are prepared to believe that the French troubadours studied metrics in Clonmacnois and Armagh, we are bound to assume that both poems are based on some late Latin metre. The same holds true of the other equally admired fragment about the blackbird by Belfast Lough. Professor Murphy attributes a very early date to two poems, 'King and Hermit' and 'May Day', which have defeated us, but in both poems the metrical system seems later than eighth or ninth century. 'May Day' is clearly linked with another poem on summer, which we have printed, and this contains an echo of some dance rhythm with three strong beats at the end of a line.

> *Fúam ngáeth mbáeth i mbruig*
> *Dairi duib Druim Daill;*
> *Rethid graig máel múad*
> *Diambi dín Cúan Caill.*

This seems to be varied by verses with an extra syllable in each line so as to produce a waltz-like rhythm.

Wanton winds blow shrill
   In the Drumdell trees;
Bald stags skip round
   Through the woods with ease.

Green bursts out everywhere;
   Oakwoods are full of leaf;
Summer's come, winter's gone;
   Stags find the briers' grief.

And the woods' wise lord,
   The bold blackbird sings;
Weary, wild, water rests
   And the salmon springs.

Sunlight all round proclaims
   Goodbye to seasons drear;
Hounds call and deer in pack;
   Ravens thrive, summer's here!

On the evidence, it would seem that nature poetry developed at some time about the tenth century as a result of hints in contemporary Latin verse, and was fostered by literary scholars who delighted in the metrical games it enabled them to play.

III

Literary scholarship eventually resulted in the arid correctness of classical Irish poetry, but in the work of the eleventh and twelfth centuries the tradition is still very much alive. The tradition was that of the amateur. To the Irish monks, even when they were professional poets, as many of them were, poetry was an amateur occupation, as it became again in the sixteenth century among members of the aristocracy. Again and again that amateur, personal note rings out even in highly polished professional verse, and a poem like 'The Blackbird', which must have been written so very late in our period that it could be regarded as classical verse is as much an early Irish poem as 'The Scholar and his Cat'.

One can find this note even in the poems of Mael Ísu Ó Brolchán, the best-known religious poet of the eleventh century. Except for one fine hymn to St. Michael, most of his verse is tedious enough, but Professor Carney has identified him as the author of two poems written in some Munster monastery by an Ulster poet who had retired there to die. Mael Ísu, in fact, did die in Lismore in the year 1086. The first is a brilliant poem on the rediscovery there of the Psalm-book he had used as a boy; the other a 'Grace before Death' written after he had suffered six months of torment.

Nevertheless the letter killed. One of the best-known of twelfth-century poems is Grania's 'Lullaby' for her lover, Díarmait, which Yeats turned into a beautiful lullaby of his own. Nature poetry here, as in another famous poem, 'A Winter Night', has become merely a background, but what indicates that this is a poetic tradition nearing its end is the historical litany of the great lovers of Irish history. This was to become a standard convention of classical poetry. In another twelfth-century poem, Cormac mac Cuileannáin, the scholarly king of Munster, is described as rejecting his wife because of his supposed connection with the Church, and he solemnly lists the saints who came chaste from their encounters with women — John, Finnbarr, Cíarán, Scuithín, Colum Cille, Mo Laise, and Patrick. In a still sillier poem a girl is comforted for the loss of her pet goose by a list of great Irish heroes who had also died, and we find a seventeenth-century version of the same theme in the poem translated by Mangan, 'The Woman of Three Cows'. The antiquarianism which was at the same time the theme and the plague of Irish literature had reasserted itself, and by the beginning of the twelfth century we are intellectually back at the end of the sixth.

IV

These poems we have edited for the general reader only, and consulted only our own pleasure in the poetry when deciding which poems to include and which verses to omit. The Irish text has been normalized into a form appropriate to the date of each poem; it should not present too much difficulty to the student equipped with the Royal Irish Academy's *Dictionary of the Irish Language*, whose system of abbreviations we have used in the short references we have given. All but one of the poems have been edited elsewhere — the majority by Kuno Meyer, whose combination of flair and scholarship first brought early Irish poetry to the notice of the outside world — and this has allowed us a freedom in emendation that would be inappropriate in a purely scholarly work.

I

HYMN TO ST. COLUM CILLE

It is just over fourteen hundred years since Colum Cille set sail for Scotland, and it seems likely that this noble hymn, from which we have selected some verses, was written in the following century, since it mentions Mo Chumma, or To Chumma, as Abbot of Iona; this kinsman of the saint returned to Ireland about 661. Note the indignant way in which the hymn-writer repudiates the charge that the saint exiled himself as penance for his part in the battle of Cúl Dremne. As well as a strict rhyme scheme the hymn has chain alliteration of an archaic kind — that is to say, the last word of each line alliterates with the first stressed word (or, occasionally, simply with the first word) of the following one.

The hymn will repay patient reading, because it contains some of the greatest lines in Irish poetry:

> Let me, while in Colum's care,
> Be guarded by the heavenly throng;
> When I tread the path of fear,
> I have a leader, I am strong.

> Fo réir Choluim céin ad-fías
> find for nime snáidsium secht;
> sét fri úathu úair no tías
> ní cen toísech, táthum nert.

Nípu fri coilcthi tincha
  tindscain airnaidi cassa;
crochais, nípu i cinta,
  a chorp for tonna glassa.

Gabais a adamrae ae,
  is coir Mu Chumma i nÍ;
is mó imrádud cech aí
  ando-rigéni in Rí. . . .

Do-ell Érinn, ind-ell cor,
  cechuing noïb nemed bled;
brisis tólae tendas for,
  fairrge al druim dánae fer.

Fích fri colainn catha líuin,
  légais la suíthi ecnae n-óg;
úagais, brígais benna síuil;
  sruth tar fairrge, flaith a lóg.

Lessach línmar, slán co céill,
  curchaib tar sál sephtus cló;
Colum Cille, caindel Néill,
  ní fríth i curp cumma dó.

Dánae arbor assa chrúas
  clér co n-imlúad aingel cert;
cemtis buidir, bathus clúas,
  cemtis luibir, bathus nert. . . .

Coluim Chille céin do-bó
  bid mo dúchann, dál co feirt;

fri cach ngúasacht géra dó,
    dath a molto mét mo neirt.

Ní gairm fri fás fil form gein,
    gigsea dom Día dúais mo bláith;
bérthum sech ríg trebas tein,
    tar sin is for fil mo ráith.

Rígdae bráthair, búadach ríg,
    rathmar fíadu feib ron ain;
eblaid goiste ndemno dím
    dúbart a baird bés dom-air.

As long as I speak under the obedience of Colum, may the fair one escort me past the seven heavens; when I go the path of terrors it is not without a leader — I have strength.
  It was not on soft beds that he undertook hard vigils; it was not for his sins he crucified his body on the blue waves.
  He made a marvellous claim; it is right that Mo Chumma should be in Iona. Greater than any man can think is what the king has done for him. . . .
  He turned aside from Ireland, he made his covenant, he crossed in ships the whales' sanctuary. He broke the wave that pressed on him, a bold man over the sea's ridge.
  He fought bitter battles with the flesh, he read pure wisdom with masters; he sewed and hoisted the tops of sails — across the current of the sea a kingdom was his reward.
  Lucky and numerous, a whirlwind swept them safely across the sea in curraghs — Colum Cille, candle of Ireland, none like him was ever found in human body.
  Bold the band whose bravery is his, a priesthood moving about

like true angels. *Though they might be deaf, he was hearing to them, though they might be sickly, he was strength to them....*

My song shall be Colum Cille's as long as he shall exact it, a bounteous interchange; in every danger I shall call on him, with all my strength I shall praise him.

What is on my lips is no cry in the desert, I shall pray God for my hero's reward; because of that he is my guarantee that he will carry me past the king who inhabits the fire.

May the royal brother, a conqueror of kings, the gracious lord, protect us with his power; he will drive away the snare of the devil from me, the supplication of his poet will perhaps protect me.

¶ From NLI Gaelic MS. 50. The poem, which has not hitherto been published, has twenty-five quatrains; the text printed here embodies a number of emendations that David Greene hopes to justify in a forthcoming edition.

2

JESUS AND THE SPARROWS

The metrical version of the 'Apocryphal Gospel of St. Thomas' edited by Professor Carney is one of the most delightful things in early Irish. The language is used with a sort of morning freshness that reminds us of some of the early English carols.

  Imbu maccán cóic blíadnae
   Ísu macc Dé bí,
  sénais dá uiscén deac,
   arrus-fí di chrí.

  Delbais dá énán deac —
   Paisir a n-anmann —
  Dia Sapaite dos-géni
   di chrí cen madmann.

  Con-saíd alaile Iudea
   Ísu mac Dé máir;
  dochum a aiti Ioseph
   don-indnacht ar láim.

  'Ergair do macc, a Ioseph;
   ní maith a ndo-gní;
  Dia Sapaite dos-rigni
   delba én di chrí.'

  Con-ort Ísu a dí bais,
   a guthán ro-cloth;

fiad a súilib — ségdae rath —
ind.énán, fos-mboth.

Ro-clos guthán cain inmain
for giun Ísu glain:
'Ar fessid ciab dergéni
airciub do for ndaim.'

Fásaig alaile do túaith,
Ba hamrae a scél,
Ro-clossa for luamain
Garmann inna n-én.

When Jesus, son of the living God, was a little boy of five years old he blessed twelve pools; he had fenced them in with clay.

He shaped twelve little birds — they are called passeres; *he made them on the Sabbath faultlessly from clay.*

A certain Jew attacked Jesus, son of the great God; he took him by the hand to his foster-father, Joseph.

'Restrain your son, Joseph; he behaves ill; on the Sabbath he made images of birds from clay.'

Jesus clapped his two hands; his little voice was heard. Before their eyes — a happy gift — he scattered the little birds.

A dear and lovely little voice was heard on the mouth of pure Jesus.

'That you may know who made you, go back to your home.'

Another proclaimed to the people; wonderful was his news; the cries of the birds were heard in flight.

¶ Text of the unique NLI Gaelic MS. 50, printed by James Carney, ITS, XLVII, 90–92.

3
JESUS AT SCHOOL

Another extract from the same poem.

Sích in suí Sacharias:
   'Amrae macc in so;
má for-cantae bed amru
   fri sodain da-no.'

Beirthi lais Sacharias
   dochum a scuile
ara ngabad légend lais
   amail cach nduine.

Ó ro scríb abbgitir dó
   as-bert 'Epir Á';
cenid frecart Macc ind Ríg
   ro-fitir ba má.

Fergaigistir maigistir,
   bí-i tar a chenn,
cia de dó tecomnacuir
   imbu dorn fa crann.

'Is é a bés,' ol Ísu,
   'nach indéuin benar
for-cain in cách noda ben
   nach sí for-canar.'

'A for-roíchan do chách,
  a rro scríbais dom,
inna llitre do-rímis
  ro-fetor a son.'

Do-rím Ísu a litre
  doaib ar a súil,
cach aí diib co n-a son
  ocus co n-a rúin.

Sích in suí Sacharias:
  'Beirith in macc úaim;
ním thá folad do fhrecrai —
  a maccán, nám lúaid.

Said the wise Zacharias: 'This boy is wonderful. He would be more wonderful still if he were taught.'

Zacharias took him with him to his school so that he might study reading with him like everyone else.

When he had written an alphabet for him he said, 'Say A. Though the Son of the King did not reply he knew more.

The master got angry; he struck him on the head, however it happened, with his fist or a stick.

'It is the custom,' said Jesus, 'any anvil that is struck teaches the one who strikes it; it is not itself that is taught.

'What you taught everybody, what you wrote for me — the letters you recounted — I knew how to pronounce them.'

Jesus recited his letters for them before their eyes, each with its sound and with its meaning.

Said the wise Zacharias: 'Take the boy away. I am not capable of answering you — boy, do not rouse me!'

4

BREASTPLATE NUMBER ONE

This poem, sometimes known as St. Patrick's *Lorica*, or Breastplate, has nothing to do with the saint, though many writers, including, regrettably, one of the editors of this volume,[1] have been led astray by the tradition. It is an eighth-century composition, intended for use as a charm before a journey, and is in the old rhythmical style. Some of its allusions are scarcely orthodox; if it is compared with the following poem, it will be seen that what we have here is a Christian breastplate with druid ornamentation, while the other is a druid breastplate with Christian ornamentation. Taken together, the two poems give a remarkably vivid picture of men's minds in eighth-century Ireland.

A breastplate is something that is bound on, and the opening word *atom-riug* means 'I gird myself'. Many years ago Ascoli pointed out that *atom-riug* could also mean 'I arise', and most translators since then have been led astray by this suggestion. But the older interpretation is better, both literally and metaphorically.

    Atom-riug in-diu
       niurt tríun
       togairm Tríndóite
       cretim treodatad
       foísitin oendatad
       i nDúilemon dáil.

[1] See Myles Dillon (ed.), *Early Irish Society* (Dublin, 1954), 27.

Atom-riug in-diu
   niurt gene Chríst cona baithius
   niurt a chrochtho cona adnacul
   niurt a esséirgi cona fhresgabáil
   niurt a thoíniuda fri brithemnas mbrátho.

Atom-riug in-diu
   niurt gráid Hiruphin;
   i n-aurlattaid aingel
   i frestul archaingel
   i frescisin esséirgi ar chenn fochraicce
   i n-ernaigdib úasalathrach
   i tairchetlaib fáthe
   i praiceptaib apstal
   i n-iressaib foísmedach
   i n-enccai noebingen
   i ngnímaib fer fírían.

Atom-riug in-diu
   niurt nime
   soilsi gréine
   étrochtai ésci
   áini thened
   déini lóchet
   lúaithi gaíthe
   fudomnai maro
   tairismigi thalman
   cobsaidi ailech.

Atom-riug in-diu
   niurt Dé dom lúamairecht:
   cumachtae nDé dom chumgabáil

cíall Dé dom imthús
rosc nDé dom remcisin
clúas Dé dom étsecht
bríathar Dé dom aurlabrai
lám Dé dom imdegail
intech Dé dom remthechtas
scíath Dé dom immdítin
sochraite Dé dom anacul
ar intledaib demnae
ar aslaigib dúalchae
ar airrechtaib aicnid
ar cach nduine mídúthrastar dam
   i céin ocus i n-ocus
   i n-úathad ocus i sochaidi.

To-cuiriur etrum in-diu inna huli nert-so
   fri cach nert n-amnas fris-taí dom churp ocus dom
      anmain
   fri tairchetla saebfháthe
   fri dubrechtu gentliuchtae
   fri saebrechtu eretecdae
   fri imchellacht n-idlachtae
   fri brichtu ban ocus gobann ocus druad
   fri cach fiss ara-chuili corp ocus anmain duini.

Críst dom imdegail in-diu
   ar neim
   ar loscud
   ar bádud
   ar guin
      condom-thair ilar fochraicce.

Críst limm, Críst reum, Críst im degaid
Críst indium, Críst íssum, Críst úassum
Críst dessum, Críst túathum
Críst i llius, Críst i ssius, Críst i n-érus
Críst i cridiu cach duini rodom scrútadar
Críst i ngiun cach oín rodom labrathar
Críst i cach rusc nom dercadar
Críst i cach clúais rodom-chloathar.

Atom-riug in-diu
   niurt tríun
   togairm Tríndóite
   cretim treodatad
   foísitin oendatad
   i nDúilemon dáil.

Domini est salus
Domini est salus
Christi est salus
   Salus tua, Domine, sit semper nobiscum.

Today I gird myself with a great strength, the invocation of the Trinity, belief in the threeness, confession of the oneness, on my way to meet the Creator.

Today I gird myself with the strength of Christ's birth and baptism, the strength of his crucifixion and burial, the strength of his resurrection and ascension, the strength of his descent for the Last Judgement.

Today I gird myself with the strength of the order of the cherubim, in the obedience of the angels, in the service of the archangels, in the expectation of resurrection to reward, in the prayers of the patriarchs, in the prophecies of the prophets, in the preachings of the apostles, in the testimonies of the confessors, in the innocence of the holy virgins, in the acts of just men.

Today I gird myself with the strength of heaven, the light of the sun, the brilliance of the moon, the glory of fire, the impetuosity of lightning, the speed of the wind, the profundity of the sea, the stability of earth, the hardness of rock.

Today I gird myself with God's strength to guide me: God's power to support me, God's wisdom to direct me, God's eye to anticipate for me, God's ear to hear for me, God's word to speak for me, God's hand to protect me, God's path to stretch before me, God's shield to guard me, God's host to save me from ambushes of devils, from temptations of evil, from assaults of nature, from all who wish me ill, far and near, solitary and in crowds.

I summon between us today all these powers against every merciless power that threatens my body and my soul, against the prophecies of false prophets, against the dark ordinances of paganism, against the false ordinances of heretics, against the encompassment of idolatry, against the spells of women and smiths and druids, against every skill that corrupts man's body and soul.

Christ be my guard today against poisoning, against burning, against drowning, against slaying, so that I may have great reward.

Christ with me, Christ before me, Christ behind me, Christ in me, Christ under me, Christ over me, Christ to the right of me, Christ where I lie down, Christ where I sit, Christ where I rise, Christ in the heart of everyone who scrutinizes me, Christ in the mouth of everyone who speaks to me, Christ in every eye that sees me, Christ in every ear that hears me.

Today I gird myself with a great strength, the invocation of the Trinity, belief in the threeness, confession of the oneness, on my way to meet the Creator.

¶ For text and variants, see *Thes.*, II, 354 ff.

It is difficult to decide how far the datives should be carried through; after *niurt Dé dom lúamairecht* there are nine lines where the manuscript tradition points strongly to nominatives, and we have not attempted emendation.

5

BREASTPLATE NUMBER TWO

The words *i llúirig*, 'in a breastplate', identify this composition as Christian, as do the odd bobs to the east, but almost every line reveals it as a druid spell. The extraordinary *mélange* would be complete if the otherwise unattested adjective *laisrén*, which, with Meyer, we have translated as 'radiant', were really a personal name, in which case we should have translated 'of St. Laserian'.

One line — 'Ro orthar mo richt' — is very doubtful; we have preferred a suggestion of our friend D. A. Binchy to that of Meyer, whose 'May my double be slain' is obviously impossible.

Ad-muiniur secht n-ingena trethan
dolbthae snáithi macc n-aesmar.
Trí bás úaimm ro-ucaiter,
trí aes dom do-rataiter,
secht tonna tocaid dom do-ro-dáilter.
Ním chollet messe fom chúairt
i llúirig laisrén cen léiniud.
Ní nassar mo chlú ar chel;
dom-í aes;
ním thí bás comba sen.

Ad-muiniur m'Argetnia
nád bá nád bebe;
amser dom do-r-indnastar
findruini febe.

Ro orntar mo richt
ro saerthar mo recht
ro mórthar mo nert
níp ellam mo lecht
ním thí bás for fecht
ro fírthar mo thecht.
Nám ragba nathair dechonn
Ná dorb dúrglass
Ná doel díchuinn.
Nám millither téol
ná cuire ban
ná cuire buiden.
Dom-í urchar n-amsire ó Ríg inna n-uile.

Ad-muiniur Senach sechtaimserach
con-altatar mná síde for bruinnib búais;
ní báitter mo shechtchaindel.
Am dún díthogail
am ail anscuichthe
am lia lógmar
am sén sechtmaínech.
Roba chétach, cétblíadnach,
cach cét diib ar úair.

Cota-gaur cucum mo lessa;
ro bé rath in Spiurto Noíb formsa.
Domini est salus
Christi est salus
Super populum tuum, Domine benedictio tua.

I call on the seven daughters of the sea, who shape the threads of long life. Three deaths be taken from me, three lives given to me, seven waves of plenty poured for me. May ghosts not injure me on my journey in my radiant breastplate without stain. May my name not be pledged in vain; may death not come to me until I am old.

I call on my Silver Champion, who has not died and will not die; may time be granted to me of the quality of bronze. May my form be exalted, may my law be ennobled, may my strength be increased, may my tomb not be readied, may I not die on my journey, may my return be ensured to me. May the two-headed serpent not attack me, nor the hard grey worm, nor the senseless beetle. May no thief attack me, nor a company of women, nor a company of warriors. May I have increase of time from the king of all.

I call on Senach of the seven lives, whom fairy women suckled on the breasts of good fortune. May my seven candles not be quenched. I am an invincible fortress, I am an unshakable cliff, I am a precious stone, I am the symbol of seven riches. May I be the man of hundreds of possessions, hundreds of years, each hundred after another. I summon my good fortune to me; may the grace of the Holy Spirit be on me.

¶ Edited by Kuno Meyer from the two MSS. (Laud 610 and BB) in *Miscellany presented to John Macdonald Mackay* (Liverpool, 1914).

6

THE NATIVITY

Bláthmacc, an eighth-century poet, retold the Biblical story in some long poems that have been edited by Professor Carney from NLI Gaelic MS. 50, which is also the source for the first three poems in this volume. Bláthmacc has neither the artlessness of the author of poems 2 and 3, nor the artistry of Óengus (see poem 10), but he has a superb narrative sense and a sensitive and lucid style. His work has the additional interest of belonging to the movement that produced the great Scriptural crosses.

> Soer a ngein ro génair úait;
> rot rath, a Maire, mórbúaid,
>   Críst macc Dé Athar di nim
>   é ron-ucais i mBeithil.
>
> Ba súaichnid dia mbá, a bé,
> cot macc i mBeithil Iude;
>   ad-fíad aingel co cló gil
>   a gein donaib augairib.
>
> Ad-cess rétglu co mméit móir
> tairngert Balam macc Beóir;
>   ba sí do-reraid an-air
>   na trí druídea co ndánaib.
>
> Tadallsat ind fhir cen úaill
> Ierosalem co Hirúaid;

THE NATIVITY

iarmi-foachtar loc nglé
i ngénair Rí na nIudae.

As-bert Heruaid, 'Aidlid lib
dús ind fhogbaid i mBeithil;
ma ro-fessid port i mbé
tísíd conid r-adar-se.'

Inmuilled ferais in rí
do chuindchid in tairngertai,
condid tetairsed tri mrath—
nípu ar onóir ná adrad.

Iar sin fúaratar do macc
it chomair, a Mairenat,
in trí druid no rádu
ad-opartat dagdánu.

Batar é in dána tra
aurum, túis ocus mirrha;
ba coinnfe do Ísu uile
Rí ba Día, ba fírduine.

Do-fíad aingel Dé di nim
sét n-aile donaib druídib;
lotar ass slán chéill dia túaith,
ní adallsat co Hirúaith.

Ad-fíad alaile, fó chíall,
i n-aislingiu do Iosiab:
'Adall la Mairi for fecht
ocus do macc i nÉgept.

> Oc cuindchid Chríst, ba trúag se,
> ortae maccrad Beithile;
>   Herúaid cródae cen a airec
> laiss tarda fo glaschlaideb.
>
> Céin-mair in maccraid moíth maith!
> Táthus subae i mbithfhlaith;
>   táthai Herúaid, tróg delb,
> bithbrón ocus bithifern.

You gave birth to a noble child, Mary, a great gift was given to you; Christ the Son of God the Father from Heaven, it was He whom you bore in Bethlehem.

That, girl, was clear to you when you were with your son in Bethlehem of Judea. An angel with shining form announced his birth to the shepherds.

There was seen a great star which Balaam the son of Beor had predicted; it was this that guided from the east the three magi with their gifts.

The humble men went to Jerusalem to Herod; they asked for the famous place where the King of the Jews was born.

Herod said, 'Go and see if you can find him in Bethlehem; if you find out the place where he is, come back so that I may adore him.'

The king urged them to search out the promised one so that he might come upon him through treachery, not to honour or adore him.

After that the three magi I speak of found your son with you, little Mary; they brought good gifts.

The gifts were gold, frankincense and myrrh, all suitable for Jesus, a king who was God and truly man.

An angel of God showed another path to the magi; they travelled safely to their country; they did not return to Herod.

Another said — a good counsel — in a dream to Joseph: 'Go, with Mary and your son, on a journey to Egypt.'

In the search for Christ, it was sad, the boys of Bethlehem were killed; without his being found they were put to the grey sword by bloody Herod.

Happy are the tender innocent boys! They have rejoicing in the eternal kingdom; Herod, wretched man, has eternal suffering and eternal hell.

¶ Text of the unique NLI Gaelic MS. 50, printed by James Carney, ITS, XLVII, 5–8.

7
THE CRUCIFIXION

Another extract from Bláthmacc's narrative.

Láthairsit dó dig séto
ar laindi a mochéco;
   con-mescsat, gním nádbu cet,
   domblas dó ar fhínacet.

Ar-ocaib guth cain cathach
oc attach a noebathar;
   'Cair rom léicis, a Dé bí
   dom daíri, dom dochraiti?'

To-celt grían a soillsi sain,
ro coíni a flaithemain,
   luid díantemel tar nem nglas
   búiristir rían trethanbras.

Ba dorchae uile in bith,
talam for-rabai rochrith;
   oc Ísu úasail aidid
   ro memdatar márailig.

Hierosalem taithsloic dían
marbu a adnacul airchían;
   isind úair i cés Críst guin
   ba dlochtae fíal in tempuil.

THE CRUCIFIXION

To-fích sruth folo, ba tinn,
combu derg snom cach oenchrainn,
 boí crú for bruinnib betho
 i mbarraib cach prímfhedo.

Ba deithbir do dúilib Dé,
muir mass, nem nglas, talam cé
 ce imm ro-cloitis a ngné
 oc coíniud a ngalgaite.

Corp Crísti fri rinde rubae
for-roeblangair crúadgubae,
 ce no coíntis cruth bad má
 in fer triasa torsata.

Ropo ainmnetach in Rí
oc crochad a oengeindi,
 olc ro coínset cen dúiri
 dia festais a dagdúili.

Nád torchair nem ina cenn,
nácha loisc in teine thenn,
 nácha báid rían romro lir —
 níptis étruim a n-aithbir:

Nácha sloic in talam trom
cúain trúaig do-géni mórglonn,
 nádbu lúaithred popul mbras
 imm Annae, imm Chaiphas.

Cen ethaiti forsin ngráic
nó bíasta for purt Piláit
 fo bíth bíe co srogul
 Ísu cen nach n-immomun.

Dín luirgg do-géni in trú,
int airrí, ba immargu,
   lassar crochad Ísu án
   lassar soerad Bar Abbán.

As-bert 'Bid ennac ar clú
i fuil ind fhíriáin Ísu;'
   ecmaing ba bibdu cach cruth
   íar mbeith oca dílsiugud.

They offered him a parting drink, desiring that he should die soon; an unlawful deed, they mixed gall with vinegar for him.

He raised a soft reproachful voice, beseeching his holy father: 'Why, O living God, hast Thou left me to my servitude and my suffering?'

The sun concealed its proper light; it lamented its lord. A swift cloud went across the blue sky, the great stormy sea roared.

The whole world became dark, great trembling came on the earth; at the death of noble Jesus great rocks burst open.

Jerusalem suddenly cast up the dead from ancient burial; in the hour in which Jesus suffered death the veil of the temple was rent.

A fierce stream of blood boiled until the bark of every tree was red; there was blood throughout the world in the tops of every great wood.

It would have been fitting for God's elements — the fair sea, the blue sky, the earth — to have changed their appearance, lamenting their calamity.

The body of Christ exposed to the spear-thrust demanded harsh lamentation — that they should have mourned more grievously the Man by whom they were created.

The King was patient at the crucifixion of his only-begotten;

badly, if they knew, did his great elements mourn him without severity.

These were no light reproaches to them: that heaven did not fall on [the guilty], nor the fierce fire burn them, nor the great sea tide drown them,

that the solid earth did not swallow the wretched crew who committed the mighty crime, that the fickle people were not turned to ashes with Annas and Caiaphas,

that birds did not assail the homestead of Pilate, nor wild beasts his palace, since, without terror, he scourged Jesus with a whip.

It was a bad choice, it was a great error that the wretch committed, the viceroy by whom Jesus was crucified and Barabbas was released.

He said: 'My fame shall be innocent of the blood of the just man, Jesus.' Nevertheless he was guilty, since he had handed him over.

¶ For text, see ITS, XLVII, 21–25.

8

THE TWO WORLDS

Bláthmacc, retelling the Bible stories, and never taking his eyes off the object, is the born narrative poet. Only when they were writing prose — and not always then — did the early Irish write good narrative. They seem to have had an incurable tendency to lyrical excess. 'The Voyage of Bran' is typical; it is full of beautiful lyric passages, but never seems to get successfully from one place to the next. These verses are beautiful in themselves, and doubly interesting because they seem to reveal a druid doctrine. The relativity of time, matter, and identity keep on recurring in the literature. This is one example, handled by an artist.

> Caíne amrae lassin mBran
> ina churchán tar muir nglan;
> os mé, im charput ca-déin,
> is mag scothach imma-réid.
>
> Is muir nglan
> don noí brainig i tá Bran;
> is Mag Mell co n-imbud scoth
> damsa i carput dá roth.
>
> Ad-cí Bran
> lín tonn tipri tar muir nglan;
> ad-cíu ca-déin i mMaig Mon
> scotha cennderga cen on.

THE TWO WORLDS

Taitnet gabra lir i ssam
sella roisc ro shiri Bran,
   bruindit srotha srúaim di mil
   i crích Manannáin maic Lir.

Lí na fairgge fora taí,
geldath mora imme-raí,
   ro sert buide ocus glas,
   is talam nád écomrass.

Lengait iich ass di brú
a muir finn forn-aiccisiu,
   it loíg, it úain co ndagdath,
   co cairdi, cen immarbad.

Ce ad-cetha oínchairptech
i mMaig Mell co n-imbud scoth,
   fil mór di echaib ar brú
   cen suide, nád aiccisiu.

Mét in maige, lín int shlóaig,
taitnet líga co nglanbóaid,
   findshruth arcait, dreppa óir,
   fáircet fáilti cech imróil.

Cluiche n-aímin, indel áig,
aigtit fri findimmarbáig
   fir is mná míni, fo doss,
   cen pheccad, cen immorbus.

Is íar mbarr fedo ro sná
do churchán tar indrada,
   fid fo mess i mbí gnöe
   fo braini do beccnöe.

> Fid co mbláth ocus torad
> for mbí fíno fírbolad,
>   fid fil cen erchra, cen bath,
>   fors fil duille co n-órdath.
>
> Fil dún ó thossuch dúile
> cen aís, cen coirbthi úire;
>   ní frescam di meth angus;
>   nín táraill in immorbus.

It seems to Bran a marvel of delight in his curragh on a clear sea. To me in my own curragh it is a flowery plain that I ride about.

It is clear sea to the beaked ship in which Bran is. In my two-wheeled chariot it is Mag Meall with many blossoms.

Bran sees a mass of waves that break over the clear sea. In Mag Mon I see crimson-headed flowers without blemish.

Sea-horses shine in summer as far as Bran's eye stretches. Flowers — streams of honey gush forth in the land of Manannán, son of Ler.

The glittering of the sea on which you are, the brightness of the sea on which you row, has poured forth yellow and blue — it is solid land.

Salmon leap from the womb of the white sea you look on; they are calves, they are lambs of good colour, in peace without slaughter.

Though you see but one charioteer in Mag Meall with its multitude of flowers, there are many horses on its breast, besides, which you do not see.

The size of the plain and number of the host shine triumphantly, a white stream of silver, a stair of gold, cause joy at every feast.

A noble arrangement, they play pleasant games in innocent conflict, men and gentle women, under the boughs, without blame, without original sin.

It is along the top of a wood that your little boat has sailed across the ridges — a beautiful wood under its harvest beneath the prow of your small boat.

A wood with blossom and fruit with the true smell of the vine on it; a wood without decay or death and with leaves of golden colour.

From the beginning of creation we are without age, without corruption of the earth; we expect no loss of strength from decay for original sin has not touched us.

¶ We have followed for the most part the text established by A. G. Van Hamel, *Immrama* (Dublin, 1941), 14-15.

9
THE NUN OF BEARE

The difficulties of this great poem have been discussed in the Introduction; having failed to arrange the verses in a satisfactory order, we print them, as Meyer and Murphy did, in the order in which they occur in the most important manuscript. We have, however, omitted some verses that can hardly have belonged to the original poem.

Aithbe dam cen bés mora
 sentu fom-dera croan;
toirsi oca cia do-gneo
 sona do-tét a loan.

Is mé Caillech Bérri Buí,
no meilinn léini mbithnuí;
 in-diu táthum dom shéimi
 ná melainn cid aithléini.

It moíni
cartar lib, nídat doíni;
 sinni, ind indbaid marsaimme
 batar doíni carsaimme.

Batar inmaini doíni
 ata maige 'ma-ríadam;
ba maith no mmeilmis leo
 ba bec no maitis íaram.

THE NUN OF BEARE

In-diu trá caín-timgarat
  ocus ní mór non aithet;
cíasu bec do-n-indagat
  is mór a mét no maithet.

Carpait lúaith
ocus eich no beirtis búaid,
  rom boí denus tuile díb —
  bennacht for ríg roda úaid.

Tocair mo chorp co n-áigthe
dochum adbae díráichne;
  tan bas mithig la Mac nDé
  do-té do brith a aithne.

Ot é cnámacha coela
  ó do-éctar mo láma —
ba inmain dán do-gnítis,
  bítis im ríga rána.

Ó do-éctar mo láma
  ot é cnámacha coela,
nídat fíu turcbáil, taccu,
  súas tarsna maccu coema.

It fáilti na ingena
  ó thic dóib co Beltaine;
is deithbiriu damsa brón:
  sech am tróg, am sentainne.

Ní feraim coirm maith milis,
  ní marbtar muilt dom banais;
is bec is líath mo thrilis,
  ní líach drochcaille tarais.

Ní olc liumm
cia beith caille finn form chiunn;
 boí mór meither cech datha
 form chiunn oc ól daglatha.

Ním-gaib format fri nach sen
inge na-mmá fri Femen;
 messe, rom miult forbuid sin,
 buide beus barr Femin.

Lie na Ríg i Femun,
Caithir Rónáin i mBregun,
 cían ó ros-síachtar sína;
 a lleicne nít senchrína.

Is labar tonn mora máir
ros gab in gaim cumgabáil;
 fer maith, macc moga, in-diu
 ní frescim do chéilidiu.

Is mó láu
nád muir n-oíted imma-ráu;
 testa már mblíadnae dom chruth
 dáig fo-rroimled mo chétluth.

Is mó dé
damsa in-diu cen buith té;
 gaibthi m'étach cid fri gréin
 do-fil aes dom aithgin féin.

Sam oíted i rrabamur
do-miult cona f hagamur;
 gaim aís báides cech nduine
 dom-ánaic a fhochmuine.

Ro miult m'oítid ar thuus;
   is buide lemm ron gleus,
cid bec mo léim dar duae
   nípa nuae in bratt beus.

Is álainn in bratt úainni
   ro scar mo Rí tar drummain;
is saer in Fer nod lúaidi,
   do-rat loí fair íar lummain.

Am minecán, mon-úar dam,
   cach derc caín is erchraide,
iar feis fri caindlea sorchai
   bíthum dorchae derthaige.

Rom boí denus la ríga
oc ól meda ocus fhína;
   in-diu ibim medguisce
eter sentainni crína.

Rop ed mo choirm cóidin meidg
ropo toil Dé cecham-theirb;
   oc do guidisiu, a Dé bí,
do-rata cró clí fri feirg.

Ad-cíu form bratt brothrach n-aís;
ro gab mo chíall mo thogaís;
   líath a finn ásas trim thoinn
is samlaid crotball senchroinn.

Rucad úaimse mo shúil des
dia reic ar thír mbithdíles;
   ocus rucad int shúil chlé
do fhormach a fhoirdílse.

Tonn tuili
  ocus ind í aithbi áin;
a ndo-beir tonn tuili dait
  beirid tonn aithbi as do láim.

Tonn tuili
  ocus ind aile aithbi,
dom-áncatarsa uili
  conda éolach a n-aithgni.

Tonn tuili
nícon toracht mo chuili;
  cid mór mo dám fo-déine
  fo-cress lám forru uili.

Ma ro fiad Macc Maire
  co mbeth fo chlí mo chuile,
ceni dernsa gart cenae
  ní érburt 'nacc' fri duine.

Tróg n-uile —
doíriu dúilib in duine —
  nád ndéccas a n-aithbe-se
feib dorr-éccas a tuile.

Céinmair insi mora máir,
dosn-ic tuile íarna tráig;
  os mé, ní frescu dom-í
  tuile tar ési n-aithbi.

Is súaill mo mennat in-diu
ara taibrinnse aithgniu:
  a n-í ro boí for tuiliu
  a-tá uile for aithbiu.

Ebb to me, unlike the sea's; old age makes me bleed. Though I may grieve at it, happily does its tide return.

I am the Nun of Béarra Baoi. I used to wear a shift that was always new. Today I have become so thin that I would not wear out even an old shift.

It is riches you love, not people; when we were alive, it was people we loved.

Dear were the people whose plains we ride about; we suited them well, and it was little they let us off.

Today they ask nicely, and it is not much they will pay back; although they give little, they let us off a lot.

Swift chariots and horses that won the prize, once I had plenty of them — God rest the king who gave them.

My body fearfully seeks its way to the house of judgement; when the Son of God thinks it time, let Him come to take his loans.

Bony and thin are my hands; dear was the trade they practised, they would be around splendid kings.

Bony and thin are my hands; I swear they are not worth raising above pretty boys.

The girls are joyous when May approaches. Sorrow is more fitting for me; I am not only sad, but an old woman.

I pour out no good sweet ale, no wethers are killed for my wedding; my hair is grey and scanty, it is no loss to have a miserable veil over it.

I do not care if there is a white veil on my head; I had coverings of every colour on my head when I drank good ale.

I do not envy anything old except Femen; while I have gone through old age Femen's crown is still yellow.

The King's Stone in Femen, Rónán's fort in Bregon, storms have long since reached them, but their cheeks are not old and withered.

The wave of the great sea is noisy, winter has stirred it up; I do not expect nobleman or slave's son to visit me today.

It is many a day since I sailed on the sea of youth; many years of my beauty have departed because wantonness has spent itself.

It is many a day since I have been warm; I have to take my shawl even in sunlight, for old age sets on one like me.

Youth's summer that I knew I have spent with its autumn, wintry age that smothers everyone has begun to approach me.

I wasted my youth to begin with, and I am glad I decided it thus; even if I had not been venturesome, the cloak would now be new no longer.

Beautiful is the distant cloak which the King has thrown over the hillside; the fuller who has covered its bareness is a craftsman

God help me! I am a poor wretch; each bright eye has decayed. After feasting by bright candles, I am in the darkness of a wooden church.

I have had my time with kings, drinking mead and wine; today I drink whey and water among withered old women.

Let my ale-feast be a cup of whey, let all that vexes me be counted God's will. Praying to you, O God, may my body's blood turn from anger.

I see on myself the shaggy cloak of age — no, I am wrong: grey is the hair that grows through my skin, like the lichen on an old tree.

My right eye has been taken away, alienated for my forfeited estate, and the left eye has been taken to complete its bankruptcy.

The flood wave, and the swift ebb; what the flood brings to you the ebb carries out of your hand.

The flood wave, and the following ebb; both have come to me, so that I am well acquainted with them.

The flood wave has not reached my pantry; though my own visitors be many, a hand has been laid on them all.

Well might the Son of Mary spend the night and be under the roof-tree of my pantry; though I am unable to offer any other hospitality, I have never said 'No' to anybody.

God help anybody — man is the most miserable of creatures — whose ebb was not seen as his flood was seen.

Happy is the island of the great sea, for the flood comes to it after the ebb; as for me, I expect no flood after ebb to come to me.

My dwelling is miserable today, so that I should recognize this: what was flooding is now all ebbing.

¶ Full MS. readings are given in Gerard Murphy's edition in *PRIA*, LV, C, 83–109. While we have assumed that the original poem was composed in the Old Irish period, we have not in every case been able to restore the appropriate forms.

10
INVOCATION TO THE MARTYRS

Óengus, who wrote about the year 800 — give or take a few years — was the greatest artist of early Irish poetry. He compiled a calendar of saints and martyrs that can only be described as infernally dull, but he was so pleased with his own labours that he wrote a Prologue and Epilogue, both of extraordinary beauty. Óengus was a popular poet who was at the same time master of every device of the schools — a Kipling trained by Horace — and has to be read aloud. The metre is very tricky and goes something like this:

> No weakling could follow
> > The pathways they followed;
> Before they were hallowed
> > All evil they swallowed.

> Sén, a Chríst, mo labrae,
> > a Choimmdiu secht nime!
> dom-berthar búaid léire
> > a Rí gréine gile.

> A gelgrían for-osnai
> > ríched co mméit noíbe,
> a Rí con-ic aingliu
> > a Choimmdiu na ndoíne!

INVOCATION TO THE MARTYRS

A Choimmdiu na ndoíne!
   a Rí fírén fírmaith!
condom roib cach solud
   ar molud dot rígraid.

Do rígrad no molur
   ol is tú mo ruiri;
do-ralus ar m'airi
   gréschi oca nguidi.

Guidiu itge doaib
   rom ain a ndo-rogbus —
caín popul co llígdath
   ind rígrad im-rordus.

Im-rordus in rígraid
   immon ríg ós nélaib,
aill ós laithib lígaib,
   aill fo díanaib déraib.

Dom-rorbae domm théiti,
   ol am tríamain trógsa:
íar timnaib ind rígsa
   rith ro ráith in slógsa.

Ro selgatar rótu
   nád soraid la baethu;
réna techt don rígu
   ro dámatar saethu.

Ro sonnta fiad slógaib
　　ot é cona mbrígaib;
ro bruithea i ndálaib
　　ro orta fiad rígaib.

Ro ringthea co rrindib;
　　ro teinntea i rrandaib;
ro loiscthea ós teintib
　　for lúachthétib lannaib.

Ro laithea for bíasta
　　la berga cen enech;
sroiglithea, séol calad,
　　tresna surnu tened.

Do-uctha a carcraib
　　i crocha a-sennad,
int shlóig oca sinnad,
　　iarna foebraib fennad.

Fáilti fri cech n-aidid
　　asa fortrén fiam;
fo-damtis, án croan,
　　már di ríagaib riam.

Ro dámatar uili
　　núallsa, mór ngním ngaile,
ar fhírthuillem mbuide
　　fri Ísu mac Maire.

INVOCATION TO THE MARTYRS

>Mairg cách roda ortsom,
>ro-lámair a nguinsom,
>iarna saethur gairseom
>ot é céin nos mairseom.

O Christ, bless my utterance! Lord of the seven heavens! Give me the gift of diligence, King of the bright sun!

Bright sun who lights heaven with all its sanctity, King who rules the angels, Lord of the people.

Lord of the people, just and faithful King, grant me all favour for the praising of your kingly household.

Your household that I praise because you are my King — I set my mind on always praying to it.

May what I have undertaken protect me, I urge my prayer on them, the lovely people with shining colour, the kingly household I have commemorated.

I have commemorated the kingly household round the King above the clouds, partly on bright days, partly in bitter tears.

May it restrain me from my wantonness, since I am but a poor wretch — the race that host ran at the behest of the King.

They hewed out roads that would have been impossible for weaklings; they suffered torments before they came to the kingdom.

For all their virtues they were flogged before hosts; they were crushed to death in assemblies; they were slaughtered before kings.

They were tortured with spears; they were torn in pieces; they were burned over fires on white-hot gridirons.

They were thrown to wild beasts by brutes without honour; they were flogged, a cruel ordeal, through blazing furnaces.

They were taken from prisons to be crucified later, mocked by the crowd when they had been flayed with swords.

Joyous at every fate whose horror is overwhelming; all the time they suffered many tortures, a noble shedding of blood.

All this lamentation they endured, a great feat of valour, to earn proper thanks from Jesus, Son of Mary.

Woe to all who killed them, all who dared to slay them, happy are they after their brief suffering.

¶ *Félire Óengusso*, 17–19. We have adopted James Carney's suggestion in the reading and translation of the last line.

11

THE DOWNFALL OF HEATHENDOM

After his celebration of the martyrs of the European Church, Óengus breaks into a marvellous passage celebrating the Irish Church of his own day, unaware that within five years it would begin to collapse under the Viking raids. In any other language but Irish these verses would be classic.

> In bith trúag i taam,
>   is duthain a ríge;
> in rí con-ic aingliu
>   is coimmdiu cach tíre.
>
> Ced a tír i taam
>   ata saidbre saigthi,
> de neurt De, delm sochla
>   fil and dún ro praidchi.
>
> At-bath borg tromm Temra
>   la tairthim a flathae;
> co llín corad sruthe
>   maraid Ard mór Machae.
>
> Ro múchad, mór tairbaid,
>   míad Loeguire roglaig;
> ainm Pátraicc án aurdairc
>   atá són for forbairt.

For-forbairt in chretem,
   méraid co dé mbrátha;
gennti bidbaid bertar,
   ni trebtar a rátha.

Ráith Chrúachain ro scáichi
   la hAilill gein mbúada;
cain ordan úas flathib
   fil i cathir Chlúana.

Classa búana binne
   im Chíarán cia at-coïs
la sessilbe mbúada
   Chlúana mór maicc Noïs,

Niptá ní bas dilsiu
   seirc Dé má do-rónaid,
adrad in ríg nélaig
   is de ní bet brónaig.

Borg Ailline úallach
   at-bath lia shlóg mbágach;
is mór Brigit búadach,
   is cain a rrúam dálach.

Dún Emna ro tetha
   acht mairde a clocha;
is rúaim iarthair betha
   Glend dálach Dá Locha.

Lóichet lainnrech lígach
    Ferna fortrén éobail;
ní mair in drong úabair
    Ráith Bécce maicc Éogain.

Cid nád ndéccaid uili
    bretha in ríg cétnai?
Ní mair Bécc mac Éogain,
    mairid Aed macc Sétnai.

Senchathraig na ngennti
    imma rérad rudrad
it fássa cen adrad
    amail láthrach Lugdach.

Ind locáin ro gabtha
    dessaib ocus trírib,
it rúama co ndálaib
    co cétaib, co mílib.

Ro milled in genntlecht
    ciarbo lígdae lethan;
ro lín flaith Dé Athar
    nem, talam la trethan.

Táthunn ní as nessa
    ar ar súil, salm sobail,
de neurt Dé dían medair,
    in-díu deüd domain.

Donnchad dricc rúad rogdae
   nó Bran búadach Berbae,
ní beir dím sním lobrae
   athigid a mmemrae.

Mael Rúain iarna gairi
   grían már des maig Midi
oc a lecht co nglaini
   ícthair cnet cech cridi.

Is comiúr in Coimmdiu
   ce thúirtir a thréta,
bithtrágaid a náimtea,
   bithmáraid a gréta.

In gormríg ro múchtha,
   in Domnaill ro plágtha,
in Chíaráin ro rígtha,
   in Chronáin ro mártha.

Na mórshlébe andaig
   ro tesctha co rinnib;
do-rónta co lléce
   slébe donaib glinnib.

The sad world in which we are, its kingdoms are brief; the King who rules the angels is the lord of every country.

Even in the land where we are, where riches are sought out, we have a famous example of God's strength to preach to us.

The great settlement of Tara has died with the loss of its princes; great Armagh lives on with its choirs of scholars.

A great cutting off, the pride of Loiguire has been stifled; Patrick's splendid, revered name is spreading.

The faith has spread and will live to the Day of Judgement; wicked pagans are carried off and their fortresses unoccupied.

The fortress of Cruachan has vanished with Ailill, victory's child; a fair dignity greater than kingdoms is in the city of Clonmacnois;

Though you should tell of sweet eternal choirs about Ciarán with the triumphant clamour of great Clonmacnois—

There is nothing that is more your own than God's love if you can achieve it; you will not grieve for adoration of the King of the Clouds.

The proud settlement of Aillin has died with its boasting hosts; great is victorious Brigit and lovely her thronged sanctuary.

The fort of Emain Machae has melted away, all but its stones; thronged Glendalough is the sanctuary of the western world.

Mighty Ferns of the yew-trees is a shining and lovely light; the proud host of the fort of Bécc mac Eogain lives no longer.

Why do you not all consider the judgements of that king? Bécc mac Eogain is dead but Aed mac Sétna is alive.

Old cities of the pagans to which length of occupation has been refused are deserts without worship like Lugaid's place.

The little places settled by twos and threes are sanctuaries with throngs, with hundreds, with thousands.

Paganism has been destroyed though it was splendid and far-flung; the kingdom of God the Father has filled heaven and earth and sea.

A holy psalm, we have before our eyes a closer example of God's strength, a stern judgement, now at the world's end.

Choice, angry, bloody Donnchad or victorious Bran from the Barrow do not lift from me the sorrow of weakness when I visit their tombs.

Mael Ruain, the sun south of the plain of Meath, after his short life — by his pure tomb the wound of every heart is healed.

The Lord is just though he separates his flocks; for ever he reduces his enemies, for ever he exalts his champions.

The proud kings have been stifled, the Donals have been plagued, the Cíaráns have been crowned, the Cronáns exalted.

The great hills of evil have been cut down with spear-points, while the glens have been made into hills.

¶ Félire Óengusso, 23–27.

12

TO ST. BRIGIT

This fine old poem, of which we print some verses, echoes the work of Óengus of Clonenagh; it is thought to be by Orthanach, Bishop of Kildare, who died in the year 840. But it does not have the concentration of the Prologue; the author intends, as Óengus did, a contrast between the glory of St. Brigit's foundation at Kildare and the ruin of Alenn, but in his enthusiasm over Alenn he loses sight of his subject and remembers it again only in the concluding verses.

The Laigin he writes of were a tribe who gave their name to the whole province of Leinster, as well as to the Lleyn peninsula in Wales, but they were driven south of the Liffey by the Uí Néill of Tara, as the Ulstermen were later driven out of Fermanagh and Monaghan. The 'Liffey' of the poem is the plain that marks their new northern frontier, not 'Anna Liffey', which is merely *Aba in Lifi*, 'the Liffey river'.

Slán seiss, a Brigit co mbúaid,
 for grúaid Lifi lir co tráig;
is tú banfhlaith buidnib slúaig
 fil for clannaib Catháir Máir.

Ba móu epirt i cach ré
 airle Dé fri hÉrinn úaig;
in-diu cid latt Life líg
 ropo thír cáich ala n-úair. . . .

Ba rí Loegaire co ler,
  Ailill Áne, adbol cor;
mairid Currech cona lí
  ní mair nach rí ro boí for. ...

Ailend aurdairc, álaind fiss,
  fil mór flaithe fo a cniuss;
ba móu foscnad tan ad-chess
  Crimthan Cosrach ina criuss.

Gáir a ilaig iar cach mbúaid
  im chúail claideb, comtaig drend;
bríg a fían fri indna gorm,
  gloim a corn for cétaib cend.

Glés a hindéon cotad cúar,
  clúas a dúan di thengthaib bard,
bruth a fer fri comlann nglan,
  cruth a ban fri hoenach n-ard.

A ól meda for cach mbruig,
  a graig allmar, ilar túath,
a seinm rond di rigaib fer
  fo duilnib sleg cóicrind crúach.

A céoil binni i cach thráth,
  a fínbarc for tonngur flann,
a fross argait ordain móir,
  a tuirc óir a tírib Gall. ...

TO ST. BRIGIT

Adrad lítha ní fíu clúas,
   solud ná sén síabras bás;
is bréc uile iarna thúr
   indid Alend is dún fás.

Foglas a ngen tibes duitt
   a maig réid túaith Críchaib Cuirc,
di cach lín ron alt a úair
   do-rigni lúaith Life Luirc.

Currech Lifi lir co hor,
   Currech Sétnai, síth co ler,
is mór ríg fris-rala cor
   Currech Corpri Niöd Fer. . . .

A Brigit 'sa tír ad-chíu,
   is cách a úair immud-rá,
ro gab do chlú for a chlú
   ind ríg, is tú forda-tá.

Táthut bithfhlaith lasin Ríg
   cen a tír i fil do rúaim;
a uë Bresail maic Déin,
   slán seiss, a Brigit co mbúaid.

Sit safely, Brigit, in triumph on Liffey's cheek to the strand of the sea; you are the princess with ranked hosts above the children of Catháir Mór.

Beyond telling at any time is God's counsel for virgin Ireland. Though the shining Liffey be yours today, it was once another's land. . . .

Loegaire was king to the sea, and Ailill Ane, a great reversal. The Curragh with its beauty remains, but no king who has ruled it endures. . . .

Famous Alenn, marvellous tidings; many a king is beneath its surface. It was greater than could be told when Crimthann the Victorious was seen in its bosom.

The shout of its triumph after each victory round a tangle of swords, a fiery encounter; the strength of its mercenary bands against the great battle array, the shriek of its horns over hundreds of heads.

The music of its bent hard anvils, the sound of its songs from the tongues of poets; the fire of its men at the great contest, the beauty of its women at the high assembly.

Its mead-drinking in every household, its fine steeds, and its many tribes; its clanking of chains on men's wrists under the blades of bloody five-edged spears.

Its lovely melodies at every hour, its wineship on the blue wave, its shower of silver of great brilliance, its gold neckbands from the lands of Gaul. . . .

It is not worth listening to the worship of auguries, or of spells or prophecies that predict death, for everything when tried is a falsehood since Alenn is a deserted fort.

Bright is the smile that shines on you from the plain north of Corc's territory; Liffey of Lorc has made ashes of every generation it has reared.

The Curragh of Liffey to the brink of the sea; the Curragh of Sétna, peaceful to the sea, the Curragh of Cairpre Nia Fer has overthrown many a king. . . .

Brigit in the land I behold, where each in turn has lived, your fame has proved greater than that of the king; you are superior to them.

You have an everlasting principality with the King [of Heaven] *apart from the land where your sanctuary is. Granddaughter of Bresal son of Dian, sit safely, Brigit, in triumph.*

¶ Edited by Kuno Meyer in 1912 from the unique copy in the Book of Leinster (lines 7148-251 in the Dublin Institute for Advanced Studies edition). Apart from a few small emendations we follow Meyer's text and translation.

13

LÍADAN

The story of Líadan and Cuirithir has come down to us only in the fragmentary notes of a professional story-teller. Cuirithir was a poet and Líadan, presumably a member of one of the ecclesiastical families that developed by the seventh century, was also able to enter the jealously guarded poets' corporation. When he arrived to marry her she was already a nun. (She may be the St. Líadan who gave her name to a County Limerick church.)

Cuirithir, in turn, became a monk, but as they continued in love, they put themselves under the direction of Cummíne of Clonfert, who submitted them to a dangerous test of intimacy. Finally, angered by Líadan, Cuirithir departed on pilgrimage.

In this great lament, Líadan contrasts her own desire and her lover's: his for an earthy, hers for a heavenly marriage.

The extraordinarily swift metre, here as in the later 'Hymn to St. Michael' by Mael Ísu, gives the poem the speed of an arrow.

    Cen áinius
      in gním hí do-rigénus;
    an ro charus ro cráidius.

    Ba mire
      nád dernad a airersom
    mainbed omun Ríg nime.

LÍADAN

Níbu amlos
   dósom in dál dúthracar,
ascnam sech phéin i Pardos.

Bec mbríge
   ro chráidi frimm Cuirithir;
frissium ba mór mo míne.

Mé Líadan;
   ro carussa Cuirithir;
is fírithir ad-fíadar.

Gair bása
   i comaiteacht Chuirithir;
frissium ba maith mo gnássa.

Céol caille
   fom-chanad la Cuirithir,
la fogur fairrge flainne.

Do-ménainn
   ní cráidfed frimm Cuirithir
do dálaib cacha dénainn.

Ní chela:
   ba hésium mo chridesherc,
cia no carainn cách cena.

Deilm ndega
   ro thethainn mo chridese;
ro-fess nicon bía cena.

Joyless is the thing I have done. I have angered the one I loved.

It would be madness not to do what pleased him were it not for fear of the King of Heaven.

The tryst I desire — to escape beyond Hell into Paradise — was no loss to him.

It was a small thing that angered Cuirithir with me. I was very gentle with him.

I am Líadan; I have loved Cuirithir: it is as true as they say.

I was only a short while in Cuirithir's company. I had a good time with him.

The music of the wood sang to me when I was with Cuirithir, and the sound of the blue sea.

I would have thought no tryst I ever made would anger Cuirithir against me.

Do not hide it! He was my heart's love, though I had loved everyone else beside.

A blast of flame has pierced my heart. Most certainly, it will not endure without him.

¶ For discussion of MSS. and previous editions, see *EIL*, 208 ff. Our text differs little from his, except that we have read *dúthracar* (1s.) for *dúthracair* (3s.) of the MSS.

14

THE EX-POET

Almost as moving as Líadan's great lament is the little poem in which she speaks of Cuirithir as the 'ex-poet'. The reader must remember that in Irish one of the words for 'monk' is *athlaech*, 'ex-layman' or 'ex-warrior'. The name of Cuirithir's father was Dobarchú, 'otter', and, accordingly, she refers to him as 'the lord of the *two* grey feet'. This is characteristic of the almost perversely ingenious poetry in this great story.

The 'wooden church' probably refers to the big parish church, which in a monastery like Clonfert, where convent and monastery school stood side by side, would be the only place where the lovers could worship together.

    Carsam,ním ráinic a less
    Cuirithir int athéces:
        inmain fíadu dá coss nglass;
        bid dirsan a bithingnas.

    In lecc fri derthach an-dess
    forsa mbíd int athéces,
        meinic tíagar di im cach ndé
        fescor íar mbúaid ernaigde.

    Nícon bia aice bó
    ná dáir inna dartado,
        nícon bia cnáim do leiss
        for láim deiss ind athécis.

Cuirithir the ex-poet loved me; I got no good of it. Dear is the lord of the two grey feet — it will be sad to be without him for ever.

The stone to the south of the wooden church where the ex-poet used to be, each day I go to it often at twilight after the triumph of prayer.

He shall have no cow, or the bulling of a heifer; no thighbone shall ever rest at the right hand of the ex-poet.

¶ Published first by Meyer (see notes to 13). He translated *carsam* in the first line as 'I loved', presumably taking it as 1 pl. perfect (OIr. *ro carsam*); to this may be objected the absence of the *ro* and the fact that there are no other examples of 1 pl. used in a singular meaning in this text. If we take the text to be OIr. the translation given above is the only possible one, and there is another example of the suffixed pronoun in *baithum immarordamais*.

The second line of the last stanza reads in the MSS. *ná dairti [dartae] ná dartado*, which Meyer translated as 'nor yearlings, nor heifers'. But *dartado* is an impossible OIr. pl. of *dartaid*; we expect *dartaidi* or *dairti*. We have therefore taken it as genitive singular and emended *dairti ná* to *dáir inna*.

15

ORDEAL BY COHABITATION

St. Cummíne tests the chastity of the lovers by putting them to bed together with an acolyte between them to observe their conduct.

CUIRITHIR: Masu oenadaig as-bir
feisse dam-sa la Líadain,
méiti la laech nod fiad
ind adaig ní archriad.

LÍADAN: Masu oendadaig as-bir
feisse dam la Cuirithir,
cid blíadain do-bermais fris
boíthiunn imma-rordamais.

CUIRITHIR: *If it is one night you say I am to sleep with Líadan, any layman who spent it would see that the night was not wasted.*
LÍADAN: *If it is one night you say I am to sleep with Cuirithir, though we spent a year at it, we should still have something to commemorate.*

16

CRÉD'S LAMENT

This is another poem from the West Munster cycle, and its background is obscure. According to the prose introduction, Dínertach had come to fight for Guaire of Gort against the Uí Néill of Tara in 649 and was killed in battle; the poem was made by Guaire's daughter Créd, who had fallen in love with him. But it makes better sense if we take it that it is Guaire's wife who is speaking.

It é saigthi gona súain
cech trátha i n-aidchi adúair
    sercgoí lia gnása iar ndé
    fir a toeb thíre Roigne.

Rográd fir ala thíre
ro-shíacht sech a chomdíne
    ruc mo lí, ní lour dath,
    ním léici do thindabrath.

Sírechtach nád décainnse
Dínertach rém lécainse,
    imbi ní bíad in fechtain
    im Dínertach mac Nechtain.

Binniu laídib a labrad
acht Ríg nime noebadrad;
    án bréo cen bréithir mbraisse,
    céile tanae toebthaisse.

CRÉD'S LAMENT

Imsa noídiu robsa nár
ní bínn fri dula dodál;
ó do-lod i n-inderb n-aís
rom gab mo théite togaís.

Táthum cech maith la Gúaire
la ríg nAidne adúaire;
tocair mo menmae óm thúathaib
isin íath i nIrlúachair.

Canair i n-íath Aidne án
im thoebu Cille Colmán
án bréo des Luimnech lechtach
dianid comainm Dínertach.

Cráidid mo chride coínech,
a Chríst cháid, arrom foíded,
it é saigthi gona súain
cech trátha i n-aidchi adúair.

The assaults that kill sleep at every hour of the cold night are spears of love from the company at day's end of the man from the border of Royny's land.

Crazy love for an outlander who surpassed all his contemporaries has taken away my looks; colour is wanting. It does not let me sleep.

Alas that I did not see Dínertach before I was deserted; there would have been no danger [?] about him, about Dínertach the son of Nechtan.

Sweeter than all songs but pious adoration of the King of

Heaven was his speech — a splendid creature with no boasting word, a slender soft-sided sweetheart.

When I was a child I was modest; I went on no unprofitable journey, but since I came to the instability of age my passion has begun to trick me.

I have all good things with Guaire, King of cold Aidne, but my mind strays from my people into the land of West Munster.

In the lovely land of Aidne round the church of St. Colmán they are singing for the splendid figure from south of Limerick of the graves whose name is Dínertach.

What has been sent to me, chaste Christ, tortures my lamenting heart. These are the assaults that kill sleep at every hour of the cold night.

¶ Published from the unique manuscript, BM Harleian MS. 5280, fo. 15b, by Kuno Meyer in *Ériu*, II, 15. Our reconstruction and translation of the third verse is tentative.

17

THE SCHOLAR AND HIS CAT

The early ninth-century poem was found scribbled on a manuscript in Austria and became justly famous. The whole of the scholar's life is reflected in its gentle, meditative humour, and many scores of literary cats have since answered to the name of Pangur. It is strongly reminiscent of the poetry of Sedulius, who was on the Continent at the time, and if, as has been supposed, Sedulius spent some time in Wales on his way to Gaul, it would explain why an Irish scholar's cat had a Welsh name, for Pangur in Old Welsh means 'fuller', so that the adjective *bán*, 'white', is superfluous.

Meisse ocus Pangur Bán,
cechtar nathar fria shaindán;
   bíth a menma-sam fri seilgg
   mo menma céin im shaincheird.

Caraim-se foss, ferr cach clú,
oc mo lebrán léir ingnu;
   ní foirmtech frimm Pangur Bán,
   caraid cesin a maccdán.

Ó ro biam, scél cen scís,
i n-ar tegdais ar n-oendís,
   táithiunn díchríchide clius
   ní fris tarddam ar n-áithius.

Gnáth, úaraib, ar gressaib gal
glenaid luch i n-a lín-sam;
   os mé, do-fuit im lín chéin
   dliged ndoraid co ndronchéill.

Fúachaid-sem fri frega fál
a rosc a nglé-se comlán;
   fúachimm chéin fri féigi fis
   mo rosc réil, cesu imdis.

Faílid-sem co ndéine dul
i nglen luch i n-a gérchrub;
   i tucu cheist ndoraid ndil
   os mé chéine am faílid.

Cia beimmi a-min nach ré,
ní derban cách a chéile;
   maith la cechtar nár a dán,
   subaigthius a oenurán.

É fesin as choimsid dáu
in muid do-ngní cach oenláu;
   do thabairt doraid do glé
   for mo mud céin am messe.

Myself and White Pangur are each at his own trade; he has his mind on hunting, my mind is on my own task.

Better than any fame I prefer peace with my book, pursuing knowledge; White Pangur does not envy me, he loves his own childish trade.

A tale without boredom when we are at home alone, we have — interminable fun — something on which to exercise our skill.

Sometimes, after desperate battles, a mouse is caught in his net; as for me there falls in my net some difficult law hard to comprehend.

He points his clear bright eye against a wall; I point my own clear one, feeble as it is, against the power of knowledge.

He is happy and darts around when a mouse sticks in his sharp claw, and I am happy in understanding some dear, difficult problem.

However long we are like that, neither disturbs the other; each of us loves his trade and enjoys it all alone.

The job he does every day is the one for which he is fit; I am competent at my own job, bringing darkness to light.

¶ From a manuscript preserved in the monastery of St. Paul in Carinthia; for the text, see *Thes.*, II, 293.

18

WRITING OUT-OF-DOORS

As we know from an observer of the seventeenth century, professional poets composed in darkness, and we actually have a poem by a seventeenth-century poet rebuking another who is known to ignore this ancient rule. Osborn Bergin properly pointed out that this must be a survival from pre-Christian times when the memorizing of a poem was itself a demonstration of skill. This little poem of the eighth or ninth century, preserved in a manuscript in Switzerland, clearly shows the differences between the professionals and the amateurs of the monastic towns.

>   Dom-fharcai fidbaide fál;
>   fom-chain loíd luin, lúad nád cél;
>   úas mo lebrán ind línech
>   fom-chain trírech inna n-én.

>   Fom-chain coí menn, medair mass,
>   i mbrott glass di dingnaib doss —
>   dé bráth nom Coimmdiu coíma!
>   caín scríbaimm fo roída ross.

A wall of woodland overlooks me; a blackbird's song sings to me (praise that I shall not hide). Over my lined book the trilling of the birds sings to me.

A clear-voiced cuckoo sings to me in a green cloak of bush-tops, a lovely utterance. The Lord be good to me on Judgement Day! I write well under the woodland trees.

¶ From a manuscript in the Stiftsbibliothek of St. Gall; for text, see *Thes.*, II, 290.

19
THE DEAD LOVER

The prose introduction to this poem gives us the setting: Ailill was the leader of a Connacht warband, Fothad Canainne of a Munster one. 'Fothad's shape was more remarkable than Ailill's, but Ailill's wife was more remarkable and more beautiful than Fothad's.' So Fothad sent one of his men to woo Ailill's wife, whose name, like that of Rónán's wife in the following poem, is not told us. She held out for a great bride-price, but finally consented to go with Fothad; Ailill followed them, and Fothad was killed in battle. The woman comes to the battlefield and Fothad's head speaks to her.

The poem consists of fifty verses, but we have dropped some of the long list of the treasures that Fothad had offered to the woman to win her. The language is that of the end of the Old Irish period, and the style is very similar to that of the following poem, which is set in Leinster.

A ben, nacham shaig i-lle
ní fritt atá mo menme;
   atá mo menme co lléic
   isind immairiuc oc Féic.

Atá mo chorpán cruach
i taíb Leitrech dá mBruach;
   atá mo chenn cen nigi
   eter fíana for garbshligi.

THE DEAD LOVER

Dochtae do neuch dáiles dáil
fácbáil dála éca fri láim;
   in dáil dálta co Clárach
   tuarnecht im robánad.

Ro delbad dún, trúag ar fecht,
for Féic do-roirned ar lecht;
   immon roírad, bág mo líuin,
   tothaim la ócu ainíuil.

Ní mé m'oenur i mmúr thal
do-chúaid fordul i ndáil ban;
   ní ar aithbiur cid dit ágh,
   is duaig ar ndedendál.

Di chéin do-roacht do dáil
baí gráin for mo choicni máir;
   ma ro-fesmais bid am-ne
   ba assa ní tairiste.

Ba ó Fhothad ind othair
beirtis co úair do-rochair;
   cid am-ne, níth fri fochaid,
   ní cen folad guin Fhothaid.

Ním rumartsa m'amusrad,
fían gormainech goburglas;
   a techt i n-úire adbai
   dirsan dond éochaill amrai.

Matis ésium batis bí
do-festais a tigernai,
   mainbed tairbad báis dímair
   lemm nípad fían cen dígail.

Co a tiugdáil batar lúaith
ad-cosnaitis bidbad búaid,
   fo-cantais rainn, trom a ngáir,
   cinsit di chlainn ruirech ráin.

Ba é fíanlach seng subach
cosin aimsir i rrubad;
   arus-foet caill duileglas
   ropo coicne uilemnas. . . .

Ná tuinite aidche úath
i lleirg eter lechta cúan;
   ní fíu cobra fri fer marb;
   fot-ruim dot daim, beir latt m'fhadb.

Atot-fuigéra cech doín
nípu étach nach díchoím,
   fúan corcra ocus léine gel,
   criss arcait, ní aicde mer.

Mo shleg coícrind, gae co fí,
diamtar menci cétguini,
   cóicriuth co mbúaile umae
   tarsna toingdis derblugae. . . .

Is dúal deitsi, sét nach lac,
m'fhidchell, ata-rella lat,
   bruinnid fuil shoer for a bil,
   ní cían di shunn indas-fil.

Is mór colnae cúan rinnech
san chan imma deirginnech,
   dosn-eim dos dlúith dairbri rúaid
   i taíb ind fhirt aniar-túaid.

THE DEAD LOVER

Oca cuindchid duit co lléir
ní rop mór no labrathar;
   ní tarla celtair talman
   tar dúil badid n-amrathar. . . .

Ataat immunn san chan
mór fodb asa forderg bal;
   dremun inathor dímar
   nodus nig an Morrígan.

Don-árlaid, dobail oígi,
is sí cotan-assoídi;
   is mór di fhodbaib niges
   dremun in caisgen tibes.

Ro lá a moing tar a ais;
cride im aithrecht noda ais;
   cid gar di shunn úann i mbé
   ná fubthad úaman do gné.

Mad co se dam fri gábud
ní gaibthi frimm do shnádud;
   a banscál, not gaib for dol,
   caín bláth fa ro scarsammor!

Scarfat fri doennacht don mud
'sin matain íar m'ócánrud;
   eirgg dot daim, sonn ní ainfe,
   do-fil deäd na haidche.

Immus-ráidfe nech nach ré
reicni Fothaid Chanainne;
   mo chobra fritt ní hinglé
   ma imráite mo thimne.

In dul bid coimtig mo lecht
ro sáitter m'ail, menn in fert,
    ní escor saítha ad-chí
    dot fhochaid íar t'inmuini.

Scarfaid frit céin mo chorp toll
m'anam do phianad la Donn;
    serc betho cé is mire
    inge adrad Ríg nime.

Is é in lon teimen tibes
imchomarc cáich bes ires;
    síabra mo chobra, mo gné,
    a ben, nacham aicille.

Do not come near to me, woman, my mind is not on you; my mind is still on the battle at Féic.

My bloody body lies beside Leitir Dá mBruach, my unwashed head is among warriors in rude slaughter.

It is arrogance for anybody to make a tryst that sets aside the tryst with death; the tryst that was made for Clara, I have come to it in deathly pallor.

Sad was my journey; it was ordained for me; my grave had been marked out on Féic. My grievous fight, it was destined that I should fall by stranger warriors.

I am not the first who went astray in the blaze of desire, trysting with women. I am not reproaching you, though you caused it — gloomy is our parting tryst.

I came from far away to meet you; it shocked my noble company. If I had known it would have been this way, it would have been easy not to persist.

Until the hour he fell it was as sick men that people were carried away from Fothad; even so, sad as the fight was, Fothad's death will not be without profit.

My war-band of noble-faced, grey-horsed warriors have not betrayed me; sad for the marvellous yew-forest to go into the house of clay!

If they were alive, their lords would be avenged; but for the hindrance of almighty death, there would be no warrior that I did not avenge.

They were swift to their final tryst, they strove to overcome their enemies; they sang a song — deep was their voice; they came of noble princely stock.

They were a swift joyous company to the moment they were killed; the green-leafed forest has received them; they were a fierce group. . . .

Do not await the horror of the night on the battlefield among the graves of the hosts. It is not worth while to speak to a dead man; go home and take my spoils.

Everyone will tell you this was not the dress of a tasteless man: a purple cloak and white tunic, a silver belt, no commonplace work of art.

My five-pointed spear, a poisonous dart that so often struck the first blow; a five-circled shield with a bronze boss on which true oaths were sworn. . . .

Yours is my chess-board — no small treasure; take it with you. Noble blood flows over its edge; it is not far away.

Many a body of the hosts of spearmen lies here and there about its frame; a tufted bush of red oak hides it beside the mound to the north-west.

Do not speak much as you search for it; earth never hid an object so marvellous. . . .

Here and there around us are many spoils of bloody appearance; frightful are the great guts the Morrigu is washing.

She has descended on us, a gloomy guest; it is she who hurls us into struggle. Many are the spoils she washes, dreadful the twisted laugh she laughs.

She has thrown her mane over her back, the heart in my former shape hates her; though she is not far from us do not let fear assail you.

Since I am in danger do not ask protection from me. Go on your way, woman; let us part while parting is fair.

Now I shall leave all human things in the morning light after my soldiers. Go home, do not wait here, the end of night is at hand.

Someone will remember my song at all times; my speech with you will not be obscure if you remember my testimony.

So that people will come to my grave, let my stone be dug in, a conspicuous monument; your labour after your love will be no waste of time for you.

My riddled body will part from you, my soul will be tortured by the death god. Earthly love is madness but for adoration of the King of Heaven.

It is the dark blackbird that laughs a greeting to all Christians. My speech, my face are ghostly. Woman, do not speak to me.

❡ Published by Kuno Meyer from the unique MS. B. IV. 2, fo. 133b, in *Fianaigecht* (Dublin, 1910), 10–21.

20

RÓNÁN'S LAMENT

This is from a Leinster saga composed probably towards the end of the ninth century. Rónán has killed his son Mael Fhothartaig, who had been falsely accused by his young stepmother (Meyer thought this derived from the Phaedra story), and Mael Fhothartaig's foster-brothers have killed her father, the King of Dunseverick, and brought back his head.

The style is much more sophisticated than that of the usual Irish saga, and the excellent verse has the same freedom from extravagance.

    Rónán: Is úar gaeth
        i ndorus tige na llaech;
          batar inmaini laích
        bítis etrainn ocus gaíth.

    Cotail, a ingen Echach,
        is mór aichre na gaíthe;
    saeth limmsa Mael Fhothartaig
        do guin i cin mná baíthe.

    Cotail, a ingen Echach,
        ní sám limm cen co tola
    aicsin Maíle Fothartaig
        inna léini lán fola.

THE WIFE: Mon úar, a marbáin chúile,
immon-rúalaid mór súile,
a ndo-ringénsam di chul
rop sí do phían iar t'athchur.

RÓNÁN: Cotail, a ingen Echach,
nídat mera na doíni;
cia broena-su do brattán
ní hé mo maccán choíni.

[She sees the head of her father, Eochaid, and kills herself.]

Ro gab Echaid oínléini
iar mbeith i leinn lebairthe;
in brónán fil for Dún nÁis
atá for Dún Sebairche.

Tabraid biad, tabraid dig
do choin Maíle Fothartaig,
ocus tabrad nech aile
biad do choin Chongaile.

Tabraid biad, tabraid dig
do choin Maíle Fothartaig,
cú fir do-bérad biad
do neoch, cid luaig no criad.

Saeth limm cúrad Daithlinne
flescaib tinnib tar toebu;
ní fil ar n-aithber fuirri,
ní sí ro rir ar coemu.

RÓNÁN'S LAMENT

Doíléne
acumsa fo-roígéne;
   a cenn for choim cáich ar úair
   oc cuindchid neich nád fogéba.

Ind fhir, ind oïc, ind eich
bítis imm Maíl Fothartaig,
   niptis formtig caemna neich
   i mbethaid a n-airchinnig.

Ind fhir, ind oïc, ind eich
bítis im Maíl Fothartaig,
   no gnítis cen cosc a-maig,
   no fertais grafainn ngraigig.

Ind fhir, ind oïc, ind eich
bítis im Maíl Fothartaig,
   Batar meinci-som úaraib
   fo ilaig iar mbithbúadaib.

Muinter Maíle Fothartaig
   cet limm cenptis desruithi;
ní maith ro gabsat oc fiur
   do-icced a n-esbuithi.

Mo mac-sa Mael Fhothartaig
   diambo adbae fid fota,
ní scoirtis cen immairi
   ríg ná rígdamnai oca.

>   Mo mac-sa Mael Fhothartaig
>   imme-réid Albain oraig,
>   ba laech etar laechradaib
>   im-beired a baind foraib.
>
>   Mo mac-sa Mael Fhothartaig
>   ba hé cuingid na cúaine,
>   éo finn fota for lassair
>   ro gab adbai co n-úairi.

RÓNÁN: *The wind is cold in the doorway of the warrior's house. Beloved were the warriors who stood between me and the wind. Sleep, Eochaid's daughter! Great is the bitterness of the wind. I grieve that Mael Fhothartaig should be killed for the sin of a lustful woman.*
    Sleep, Eochaid's daughter! I have no comfort even if you do not sleep, seeing Mael Fhothartaig in his shirt full of blood.
THE WIFE: *Alas, O corpse in the corner that eyes would linger upon. The sin I committed was your suffering after your exile.*
RÓNÁN: *Sleep, Eochaid's daughter! Men are not mad. Though you wet your cloak, it is not my son you weep.*

    ·   ·   ·   ·

    Eochaid has donned one shirt after being in a long, warm cloak; the grief that is on Naas is also on Dunseverick.
    Give food, give drink to the hound of Mael Fhothartaig, and let someone else give food to Congal's hound.
    Give food, give drink to the hound of Mael Fhothartaig, the hound of a man who gave food to all, whatever price he paid.
    I grieve to see Dathlenn beaten on the sides with hard rods. I

have no cause to reproach her; it is not she who sold my dear ones.

Doílin has served me; her head is on everyone's lap, searching for one she will not find.

The men, the youths, the horses that were about Mael Fhothartaig were anxious for no man's protection in the lifetime of their leader.

The men, the youths, the horses who were about Mael Fhothartaig, unhindered they exercised on the plain, they competed in horse races.

The men, the youths, the horses who were about Mael Fhothartaig, often did they pass with shouts of triumph after crushing victories.

Mael Fhothartaig's folk, though they were not dishonoured, ill did they support the man who came to them in their needs.

My son Mael Fhothartaig whose dwelling was the wide wood, neither king nor king's son would unyoke there without keeping watch.

My son Mael Fhothartaig who had ridden over all Scotland to its borders was a warrior among warriors and took sway over them all.

My son Mael Fhothartaig was the prop of the hunt; the long white blazing yew-tree has taken up a cold dwelling.

¶ Edited first by Kuno Meyer (*RC*, XIII, 368–97) and recently by David Greene (*Fingal Rónáin and other stories*, Dublin, 1955), from LL, 271–3, and H.3.18, 749–54.

Although the verse appears to belong to the Old Irish period, there are some rhymes (*fo-roígéne: fogéba: cúaine: úairi*) that point to a later date and which we have not been able to emend.

21

WINTER

This famous little poem from the ninth century is the last word in compression.

>   Scél lem dúib:
>   dordaid dam,
>   snigid gaim,
>   ro fáith sam.
>
>   Gáeth ard úar,
>   ísel grían;
>   gair a rrith,
>   ruirthech rían.
>
>   Rorúad raith,
>   ro cleth cruth,
>   ro gab gnáth
>   giugrann guth.
>
>   ro gab úacht
>   etti én;
>   aigrid ré —
>   é mo scél.

I have news for you: the stag bellows, winter snows, summer has gone.

The wind is high and cold, the sun is low; its course is brief, the tide runs high.

The bracken has reddened, its shape has been hidden; the wild goose has raised his customary cry.

Cold has caught the wings of birds; it is the time of ice — these are my news.

¶ See *RC*, xx, 258.

22

THE PITY OF NATURE—I

This little lyric is all that remains of a ninth-century version of the story of Suibne, an Ulster king who went mad during the battle of Mag Rath in 639 and took refuge in the woods. As one can see from it, and from the lyric we print from the twelfth-century version, Irish monastic poets tended to regard wild life as the antithesis of social life, and this tendency was almost certainly encouraged by the eremitic movement. It is highly improbable that the eremitic movement produced it. Suibne's 'oratory' is the tree in which he has made his home.

M'airiuclán hi Túaim Inbir,
   ni lántechdais bes séstu,
cona rétglanaib a réir
   cona gréin, cona éscu.

Gobbán do-rigni in sin,
   co n-écestar dúib a stoir;
mo chridecán, Día du nim,
   is hé tugatóir rod toig.

Tech inná fera flechod,
   maigen 'ná áigder rindi,
soilsidir bid hi lubgurt
   os é cen udnucht n-imbi.

A full household could not be more lovely than my little oratory in Tuaim Inbir with its stars in their order, with its sun and its moon.

That you may be told its story it was a craftsman who made it — my little heart, God from Heaven, he is the thatcher who thatched it.

A house where rain does not pour, a place where spear-points are not dreaded, as bright as in a garden and with no fence about it.

¶ From the same St. Paul MS. as number 17. For the text, see *Thes.*, II, 293.

23

ITA AND THE INFANT JESUS

St. Ita (in Modern Irish Íde) was a sixth-century Munster saint to whom, we are told, was granted the privilege of nursing the infant Jesus. An Irish poet of the old school would have raised his eyebrows at the ingenuousness of this little poem, perhaps of the tenth century, but it keeps its charm.

Ísucán
    alar liumm im dísiurtán;
cia beth cléirech co llín sét
    is bréc uile acht Ísucán.

Altrom alar liumm im thig
    ní altrom nach doerathaig;
Ísu co feraib nime
    frim chride cech n-oenadaig.

Ísucán óc mo bithmaith
    ernaid ocus ní taithbech;
in rí con-ic na uili
    cen a guidi bid aithrech.

Ísu úasal ainglide
    nocho cléirech dergnaide
alar liumm im dísiurtán,
    Ísu macc na Ebraide.

Maicc na ruirech, maicc na ríg,
   im thír cia do-ísat-án,
ní úaidib saílim sochor,
   is tochu liumm Ísucán.

Canaid cóir, a ingena,
   d'fhiur dliges bar císucán;
atá 'na phurt túas-acán
   cia beth im ucht Ísucán.

It is Jesuseen I nurse in my little hermitage. All is a lie but Jesuseen, even though it were a priest with great wealth.

The nursing that I do in my house is not the nursing of any common man. Jesus with the men of heaven lies against my heart each night.

Young Jesuseen, my eternal fortune, he bestows and does not default. The King who rules all things, it would be grievous not to pray to him.

It is noble, angelic Jesus and not any ordinary cleric that I nurse in my little hermitage — Jesus, son of the Jewess.

Princes' sons, kings' sons, though they come into my territory, it is not from them that I expect advantage; better I like Jesuseen.

Sing a chorus, girls, to the man you owe your little rent to — Jesuseen, who is in his home above although he is at my breast.

¶ For text and variants, see *EIL*, no. 11.

24

TRIADS

The triad, the simplest of all mnemonics, is the most rudimentary form of organized thought, and before the Irish learned to read and write they passed on legal and other distinctions in the form of triads and heptads. As *everything* had to be got into one or the other, we sometimes find triads of four headings, and heptads of six or eight. Students in the native schools enjoyed them as a literary exercise, as a few examples will show.

Trí gena ata messa brón: gen snechtai oc legad, gen do mná fritt iar feis la fer n-aile, gen con foilmnich.

Trí báis ata ferr bethaid: bás iach, bás muicce méithe, bás foglada.

Trí bráthair úamain: sta! sit! coiste!

Téora seithir góa: bés, dóig, toimte!

Téora seithir oíted: tol, áilde, féile.

Téora seithir sentad: cnet, genas, éitche.

Trí aithgin in domuin: brú mná, úth bó, ness gobann.

Trí as mó menmnae bís: scolóc iar légad a shalm, ocus gilla íar lécud a eiri úad, ocus ingen íar ndénum mná dí.

Trí as ansu bís do acallaim: rí imma gabáil, ocus Gall ina lúirig, ocus aithech do muin commairchi.

Trí ata ferr do fhlaith: fíu, síth, slóg.

Trí gúalae doná fess fudomain: gúalae flatha, gúalae ecailse, gúalae nemid filed.

Three smiles that are worse than grief: the smile of snow melting, the smile of your wife to you after sleeping with another man, the smile of a leaping dog.
Three deaths that are better than life: the death of a salmon, the death of a fat pig, the death of a robber.
Three brothers of terror: hush! hist! listen!
Three sisters of lying: perhaps, maybe, guess!
Three sisters of youth: desire, beauty, generosity.
Three sisters of age: a sigh, chastity, ugliness.
Three renewals of the world: a woman's belly, a cow's udder, a smith's furnace.
Three of the highest spirits: a student having read his Psalms, a servant having laid down his load, a girl having been made a woman.
Three that are hardest to talk to: a king bent on conquest, a Viking in his armour, and a low-born man protected by patronage.
Three best things for a king: merit, peace, an army.

Three vats whose depth no man knows: the vat of a king, the vat of a church, the vat of a poet's privilege.

¶ See Kuno Meyer's edition of the *Triads of Ireland* (Dublin, 1906), numbers 91, 92, 137, 136, 206, 207, 148, 233, 232, 242, 255.

25

DRAMATIS PERSONAE

It is often impossible to tell what some of the hundreds of fragments scattered through annals, textbooks, and romances really are. Number 4 is almost certainly a storyteller's verse, and perhaps also number 3; numbers 5 and 6 look like contemporary Court poetry, but what are the first two? They can hardly be as old as the events they commemorate, but why should someone hundreds of years later write such elaborate encomia?

Notice, too, that though the textbooks do not mention it, the first three are in a form that seems uniquely Irish, that of the double epigram with verses in contrasting metres.

1. *Aed macc Colggan* (d. 610)

Ro boí tan
ba linn orddan Loch Dá Dam;
   nípu é in loch ba orddan
   acht flaith Aeda maicc Colggan.

Cumma dam,
nád mair carae rodom char,
   ce bé fo-cherr trillsi treb
   tre innsi Locha Dá Dam.

2. *Aed Bennán* (d. 619)

Aed Bennán
   dind Éoganacht íar Lúachair,

is mairgg séotu díanid rí,
céin-mair tír díanid búachaill.

A scíath in tan fo-chrotha
a bibdada fo-botha;
cesu becán for a muin
is dítiu dond Íarmumain.

3. *Conaing drowned* (622)

Tonna mora mórglana
grían roda thuigsetar;
inna churchán fhlescach fhann
for Conaing con-cuirsetar.

In ben ro lá a moing find
inna churach fri Conaing;
is cas ro tibe a gen
in-diu fri bile Torten.

4. *The Dead Princes in the Mill* (650)

In grán meles in muilenn,
ní coirce acht is dergthuirenn;
ba do géscaib in chrainn máir
fotha muilinn Maelodráin.

5. *Feidilmid, King of Munster* (840)

Is é Feidilmid in rí
díarbo opair oenlaithi
aithrígad Connacht cen chath
ocus Mide do mannrad.

6. The King of Connacht

'In acabair
    Aed Connacht 'sind áth?'
'Ad-chonncamar
    cid a scíath ar a scáth.'

1. There was a time when Loch Dá Damh was a famous lake. It was not the lake that was famous, but the reign of Aed mac Colgan.

It matters nothing to me, when the friend who loved me lives no more, who builds a wattle house on the island of Loch Dá Damh.

2. Aed Bennán of the Eoghanacht of West Kerry, woe for the treasures of which he is king, happy the land to which he is herd-boy.

When he shakes his shield he scatters his enemies. Though it be small on his back it is the protection of West Munster.

3. The great clear waves of the sea have covered up the strand; they have combined against Conaing in his frail wickerwork boat.

The woman has tossed her white mane at Conaing in his curragh. It is crookedly she has smiled today at the tree of Tortu.

4. The grain the mill grinds is not oats but red wheat. The grist of Maelodrán's mill came from the boughs of the great tree.

5. Feidilmid is the king to whom it was the work of a day to unking Connacht without a battle and lay waste Meath.

6. '*Did you see Aed of Connacht in the ford?*' '*We saw only his shield protecting him.*'

¶ 1. *FM*, anno 606.   2. *FM*, anno 614.   3. *AU*, anno 621.
4. *AU*, anno 650.   5. *AU*, anno 839.   6. *IT*, III, 12, §20.

26

MEN AND WOMEN—I

Again we have no method of knowing what the origin of these verses is. Number 6 is certainly from a ninth- or tenth-century version of the story of Díarmait and Grania, and literally this is all that remains of it. Numbers 1, 8, and 9 are probably genuine epigrams.

1. *A Flatulent Woman*

A-tá ben as-tír,
   ní eprimm a hainm;
maidid essi a deilm
   amal chloich a tailm.

2. *Etan*

Ní fetar
cía lassa fífea Etan;
   acht ro-fetar Etan Bán
   nícon fhífea a hoenurán.

3. *The Goldsmith's Wife*

Ingen gobann
   ben na cerddae,
gnúis roglaisse
   is roderggae.

4. *A Kiss*

Cride é,
   daire cnó,
ócán é,
   pócán dó.

5. *Love in Exile*

Céin-mair 'na luing indfhota
   oca mbíat a lennata
oc imram ard allata
   íar n-ingnais a mennata.

6. *Grania*

Fil duine
   frismbad buide lemm díuterc,
ara tabrainn in mbith mbuide
   uile, uile, cid díupert.

7. *If I were the Girl*

Díambad messe in banmaccán
no cechrainn cach felmaccán,
   fer nád fintar co cluinter,
   slánchéill chéin dúib, a muinter.

8. *The Pilgrim to Rome*

Techt do Róim,
   mór saítho, becc torbai;
in Rí con-daigi i foss,
   manim bera latt ní fhogbai.

9. *Viking Times*

Is aicher in gaeth in-nocht,
fo-fúasna fairrge findfholt;
 ní águr réimm mora mind
 dond laechraid lainn ó Lothlind.

10. *The Bell*

Clocán binn
 benar i n-aidchi gaíthe,
 ba ferr lemm dul ina dáil
 indás i ndáil mná baíthe.

11. *Hospitality*

A Rí rinn,
cid dub mo thech nó cid finn
 nícon íadfaider fri nech
 nár íada Críst a thech frimm.

---

1. There's a woman in the country (I do not mention her name) who breaks wind like a stone from a sling.

2. I do not know who Etan will sleep with, but I do know that Blonde Etan will not sleep alone.

3. The goldsmith's wife is the blacksmith's daughter, with a face of great whiteness and great redness.

4. He's my heart, my grove of nuts; he's my boy, here's a kiss for him.

5. Happy those who have their sweethearts in a long-prowed boat, rowing off high and proud, having abandoned their country.

6. There's a man I would wish to see, for whom I would give the golden earth, all, all, though it were an empty bargain.

7. If I were the girl I would love every student — a man you can't know till you hear him talk — a long farewell to you my family!

8. To go to Rome is much labour, little profit; the King you seek there, unless you bring Him with you, you will not find Him.

9. Bitter is the wind tonight, it tosses the sea's white hair; I do not fear the wild warriors from Norway, who course on a quiet sea.

10. The sweet little bell that is struck on a windy night, sooner would I tryst with that than tryst with a lustful woman.

11. King of stars, whether my house be dark or bright, I shall shut it on none lest Christ shut his house on me.

¶ 1. See *RC*, xx, 158, §7. 2. *IT*, III, 19, §52. 3. *IT*, III, 60, §120. 4. *IT*, III, 100, §177. 5. See *Bruchstücke*, §162. 6. *LU*, 514–17. 7. *Auraicept*, 533–6. 8. *Thes.*, II, 296. 9. *Thes.*, II, 290. 10. *IT*, III, 16, §40. 11. LB, 93.

27

PARADISE REVISED

In the matter of style and melody Irish is superior to any poetry we know, but the author of *Saltair na Rann* — 'The Rhymed Psalter' — written towards the end of the tenth century, would take a high place in any literature for sheer incompetence. Like a bad swimmer he puts out tremendous effort in order to travel a few yards, and his splashing and thrashing are an entertainment in themselves. But he can also be read for the extraordinary amalgam of folk-lore, both foreign and native, that he has assembled about the Biblical narrative; the result, however unscriptural, is thoroughly Irish.

It must be explained that Adam and Eve, expelled from Paradise, have taken refuge, the former in the Jordan and the latter in the Tigris. Adam persuades the river to cease flowing, that is, to fast with him against God, just as the saints of Ireland fasted against Díarmait at Tara. The Jordan gathers all its wild life around Adam, and all invoke the nine heavenly orders to plead with God for forgiveness. When the Devil realizes that the pair are forgiven he renews his plotting. Disguised as an angel he visits Eve and pretends to bring her a message from God to leave the Tigris. When the two appear on the bank of the Jordan Adam despairingly reveals to Eve the identity of her companion.

> Mar at-chúala Eua in sain
> reba athchosain Ádaim
> dos-fuit for lár, luid i ssás,
> is bec ná dechaid díanbás.

ADAM: A Luicifeir, a Demuin,
cid 'm a-taí diar lenamuin?
　　ron gaelaigis, cían ro clos,
　　ron baethaigis i Pardos.

Ó ro scarsatar ar cuir
náchar len, a Luicifuir,
　　triat chuimleng a-tám i cacht;
　　ní chuingem do chomaitecht.

Ní sinn ro gab do maithius
nó rot chuir ót fhírfhlaithius;
　　ní sinn ro thimgair fo chlith
　　do chor do dindgnaib ríchid.

Ní sinn ro gab na sosta
bátar fout, a anfhosta;
　　ní sinn rot scar frit shlúagu
　　frit cheólu, frit ilbúadu.

Ní sinn dot-rat fo chairib
ót bruigib, ót mórmaigib,
　　condat fail fo deilb Díabail
　　tre bithu fo bithpíanaib.

Ní sinn fot-ro-glúais do nim
a anbúais, trit imresain;
　　ní sinn rot scar frit gním cain
　　ní sinn ro gab t'airmitin.

Ní sinn rot lá ót shoillsib,
fot-rochess ót mórchoimsib,
　　díandot fail fo déin toimthig
　　i mbithphéin, i mbithdorchib.

Do chomthocbáil fri Ríg recht
iar fír dot-rat i n-amnert;
   fo-fúarais mór do duilgi
   triat díummus, triat anuimli.

Cid dia taí diar fagail i fus
úair dar-ralaid o Phardus?
   Ron slatais 'm ar mbethaid nglain,
   don-ratais i comrargain.

LUCIFER: In cuman lat, a Ádaim,
na fúarus d'ulcc fot dágain?
   mo chur do maig nime náir
   mo bith fo thrúaig dígráid? . . .

In cuman lat, a Ádaim,
na fúaras d'ulcc fot dágain?
   Ní raba cen chith, cen chath,
   ón ló rodot tuistigad.

Trúag, a Ádaim, do dígail
fot dágain dún dib línaib,
   do chur-sa a brug Pharduis bil,
   is mo chur-sa do naebnim.

Ad-fia-sa duit cen bréic mbrais
órsam eólach sét senchais,
   feib léir don-ralad do nim
   messe ocus tussa, a Ádaim.

Dia tarat Día tinfed nglan
dochum do chuirp i talam
   rot delgnad fri cach dúil tinn
   in lá ro delbad t'anim.

Dia rot chruthaiged co glé
fo chosmailius deilbe Dé,
   dia n-erbrad fri cach dúil ndil
   co tíssed dot airmitin.

Diar fhaíd Día Míchél do nim
cucut sech cách, a Ádaim,
   condot ruc fo glanbad glan
   do adrad in Dúileman. . . .

Ó r' adrais Rí na recht rinn
fíadait fír foroll forfind,
   ro idpart Día cach ndúil ndein
   tre bithu frit airmitein.

Ro ráid Míchél frimm iar fír
co tísainn d'adrad ind Ríg
   cen fhuirech, cen choísed cath,
   combad mé toísech tíssad.

Iarsin do-dechad fo deóid
la forngaire maith Mícheóil
   co tarrasar fom níab glan
   i fíadnaise in Dúileman.

Ro ráidi rinn in Rí rán:
'Cluinid, a lucht na noí ngrád:
   tabraid úaib airmitiu glan
   dom chomdeilbsi, do Ádam.'

Ráidim-se fri Dia as mo thass
aithesc feochair fíramnas:
   'Nách é Ádam, érimm nglé,
   óssar na ndúile n-uile?

In córu in sinser iar sreith
do dul d'adrad int shósair,
   fo in sósar, cen dalbad ndil,
   is chóir d'adrad int shinsir?'

Ro ráid trían int shlúaig co glé
eter aingle is archaingle,
   ro forgellsat fiad cach thur:
   'Is fír fors-tá Luicifur.'

Iar sain ro ráidi guth Dé:
'Cluinte, a Luicifuir co glé,
   bid é in t-óssar bas úasal
   céin beo-sa 'co dindúasad.'

'Cia thíasat lucht noí ngrád cain
dia airmitnigud Ádaim,
   ní rag-sa dó, dígrais cruth,
   úair am siniu i tuistigud.'

Rom lá fo chétóir do nim
día, trit chinaid, a Ádaim,
   iar frittuidecht dam-sa am-ne
   fria thimne, fria fhorngaire.

Then, when Eve heard Adam's words of reproach, she fell to the ground, went into a swoon, she all but died on the spot.
ADAM: *Lucifer, devil, why are you pursuing us? You overcame us, it has been long known, and betrayed us in Paradise.*
   Since our agreements are at an end, do not pursue us, Lucifer. It is through your machinations that we are in bondage. We cannot support your company.

It is not we who took your benefits away or banished you from your true principality; it is not we who secretly devised your removal from the dwellings of Heaven.

It is not we who seized the couches from beneath you, you restless one; it is not we who separated you from your hosts, your music, your many triumphs.

It is not we who brought you under reproaches from your lands, from your wide plains, so as to bring you into the shape of the devil, suffering endlessly through eternity.

It is not we who drove you from Heaven because of your quarrelsomeness, O base man; it is not we who parted you from your great achievement; it is not we who snatched your reverence.

It is not we who tossed you from your bright places, and removed you from your great powers, so that because of it you are under stern threats in eternal pain, eternal darkness.

Truly, it was your insurrection against the King of laws that crippled you. You have suffered greatly, through your pride and your disobedience.

Why do you assault us here since we have been driven out of Paradise? You have tricked us of our lovely life, you have hurled us into error.

LUCIFER: *Do you remember, Adam, how much ill I suffered because of you? Cast out of the great plain of Heaven and living in miserable disgrace? . . .*

Do you remember, Adam, how much ill I suffered because of you? I have not gone without grief or war since the day you were created.

Alas, Adam, for the revenge you brought on both of us, yourself cast out of the fair house of Paradise and I cast out of holy Heaven.

I shall recount for you without an impudent lie since I am learned in the ways of history, Adam, exactly how you and I were thrown out of Heaven.

When God breathed the breath of life into your body on earth, from the day your soul was fashioned, you were distinguished from every stout element.

When you were clearly created in the image of God, when every beloved element was told to come and reverence you.

When Michael was sent from Heaven to you above all others, Adam, and brought you in perfect purity to worship the Creator. . . .

From the time when you worshipped the King of the clear laws, the true omnipotent, resplendent Lord, God dedicated every swift element to reverence you throughout eternity.

Michael said to me quite truthfully that I should go to worship the King without delay and without conflict since it was I who should come first.

So at last I went on the adequate summons of Michael and came in my splendour into the presence of the Creator.

The great King said to us: 'Listen, you of the nine orders, give absolute submission to my image, to Adam.'

I out of my silence offered to God a fierce wild speech: 'Is it not plain that Adam is the youngest of all created things?

'Is it more proper that the senior in rank should adore the younger, or that the younger should properly worship the elder, without guile?'

A third of the host, angels and archangels, said loudly, judging in the presence of everyone: 'Lucifer is right.'

Then the voice of God said: 'Listen properly to me, Lucifer; the youngest shall be chief as long as I am supporting him.'

'Even though the whole host of the nine orders should go to reverence Adam, it is my earnest resolve that I shall not go, because I am older in creation.'

Immediately, because of your fault, Adam, God hurled me from Heaven, for opposing myself to his will and his proclamation.

¶ *Saltair na Rann* is found uniquely in the Oxford MS. Rawlinson B, 502; it was published by Whitley Stokes in 1883. The section dealing with Adam and Eve has been discussed by St. John D. Seymour in *PRIA*, XXXVI, C, no. 7.

The meaning of the word *coísed* is unknown; following the RIA *Dictionary*, we take *dindúasad* as a compound of *dúasad*.

28

PRAYER FOR A LONG LIFE

This unusual and moving poem appears from the solitary manuscript to be in late Middle Irish. After one has worked over it a couple of times one begins to realize that it must originally have been written in Old Irish; in fact it is quoted in a glossary compiled about the year 900.

The Middle Irish form not only obscures the rhymes, but occasionally the sense as well. It is as impossible to restore the early text as it is to enjoy the later one, and all we can do is to scrape away some of the accretions and reveal something of the original brilliance.

Hence our eclectic text is neither fish nor flesh and some of it is pure guess-work.

An frimm, a Rí ríchid ráin
    comba etal fri dáil ndóig,
co clothar cach ní as-ber
    am santach sen, a Dé móir.

A Maic Maire, míad cen on,
    a mmo Choimmdiu con-icc nem,
a ruiri na n-aingel finn,
    in anfa frimm comba sen?

Ad-teoch-sa mo guidi fritt,
    ar báig Maire dianda macc —
mainbad tochrád latt, a Rí —
    do-rónainn ní bad maith latt.

Maccán berar riana reib,
    ní finntar feib ara-mbé;
is i n-oítid lenar baes,
    a gaís cen aes bés ní té.

Ní hortai loeg fri haes mer,
    cach sen is tressa a chách;
ní hortai úan, ná orc maeth,
    ní coillti craeb riana bláth.

Búain guirt résiu rob abbaig,
    cair in cacaid, a Rí rinn?
is é in longud réna thráth
    bláth do choll in tan bas finn.

Fuiniud i mmedón laa,
    ní hord baa a rían rom;
matan i n-aidchi, in dedól
    réna medón, cia mó col?

Cluinte itchi, not guidiu,
    as mo chridiu deróil dúr,
a Maicc Dé, cia nom rodbai,
    is bec torbai duitt ind úr.

Duittse, a Dé, mo tholtu,
    ceni bé sentu dom chorp;
ce nom bera cen taithlech,
    nícon bia m'aithber fort.

Is fort shnádud cacha bí;
    ré ndul i crí, a Rí shláin
oc do guidi dam cen díchil
    an frimm, a Rí ríchid ráin.

Wait for me, King of the glorious kingdom, until I am pure for the inevitable assembly. Till everything I shall say is heard, I am envious of old men, O great God.

Mary's son, dignity without blemish, my Lord who rules over Heaven, Prince of the white angels, will you wait for me till I am old?

I urge my prayer upon you for the love of Mary, whose son you are, if it be no displeasure to you, O King, so that I might do something that would please you.

A lad who is carried off before his playing time, nobody knows the excellence that may await him; it is in youth that folly is pursued, without age he may not reach his skill.

A calf should not be killed in its giddy time, for everything old grows stronger; a lamb or a sucking pig should not be killed, nor a bough plucked before it flowers.

Reaping a field before it is ripe, what sense is there in that, O King of stars? It is feasting before one's time to spoil a flower when it is white.

Sunset at midday — its premature course is no good order; morning in the night-time, daybreak before midnight, what greater sin?

Listen to a request, I pray you, from my miserable hard heart; Son of my God, even if you destroy me, clay is little profit to you.

I give you my love, O God, even if my body does not attain old age; though you cut me off without any amendment, I shall not complain of you.

Everything in the world depends on your protection. Before I go into earth, O holy King, let me be for ever praying you — Wait for me, King of the glorious kingdom.

¶ Edited from the unique MS. LL, 374c, by M. O'Daly, *Éigse*, II, 183-6.

29

THE TEMPEST

This marvellous poem is ascribed to Rumann, a famous poet who died in 748, and the story goes that he wrote it for the Norsemen of Dublin while drunk. There were no Norsemen in Dublin at that time; the poem is eleventh century, and the author was certainly not drunk. The 'rocking metre', as the metrists call it, could be used only by a man in full possession of his faculties. Through it, one can almost feel the lurch of the boat and hear the straining of timbers. Gerard Manley Hopkins' 'The Wreck of the *Deutschland*' is probably the nearest thing to this poem in English.

> Anbthine mór ar muig Lir,
> dána tar a hardimlib;
>   at-racht gáeth, ran goin gaim garg
>   co tét tar muir mórgelgarb;
> dos-árraid ga garggemrid.
>
> Gním in muige, mag Lir lór,
> ro lá sním ar ar sírshlóg;
>   écht móo cách (ni lugu);
>   cid as ingantu didiu
> in scél direcra dimor?
>
> Ó do-chuir in gáeth an-air
> menma tuinne tarcabair;

THE TEMPEST

dúthracair dul tarainn síar
cosin fót fris fuinenn grían,
   cosin glasmuir ngarglethain.

Ó do-chuir in gáeth a-túaid
dúthracair tonn temenchrúaid
   co mbad fri domun an-des,
   fri fithnem ro ferad tres,
ró ésted fri elechdúain.

Ó do-chuir in gáeth an-íar
tar in sáile srebachdían
   dúthracair dul tarainn sair
   co crann gréine coros gaib
i muir lethan leborchían.

Ó do-chuir in gáeth an-des
tar tír Saxan scíathanbres
   co mbenann tonn Inse Scit,
   do-luid do chuirr Calad Nit
co mbrut luibnech líathanglas.

Is lán ler, is lomnán muir,
is álainn in etharbruig;
   ro lá curu in gáeth gainmech
   im Inber na Dá Ainmech;
is lúath luí le lethanmuir.

Ní sádail súan, sén garg sáir,
co mbruthbúad, co mbarannbáig;
   fordath eala forda-tuig
   mag mílach cona muintir;
glúastar mong mná Manannáin.

Ro lá tonn, trén a trethan,
tar cech inber íarlethan;
   don-rocht gáeth, ron goin gaim gal,
    im Chend Tíre, im Tír nAlban
silid sreb lán slíabdreman.

Mac Dé Athar, adblib scor,
rom ain ar gráin garganfod;
   fíadu fírén na fleide
    acht rom ain ar anside,
ar Iffern co n-ardanfod.

There is a great tempest on the plain of Ler, bold over its high borders. The wind has risen, rough winter has killed us, and comes to us over the great wild sea — the spear of the wild winter has overtaken it.

The behaviour of the plain, the immense plain of Ler, has troubled our enduring host. A marvel greater than all (no less), for what is there more wonderful than the incomparable, tremendous tidings?

When the wind blows from the east the spirit of the wave is stirred; it longs to go past us westwards to the land over which the sun sets, to the blue sea, rough and wide.

When the wind blows from the north, the dark fierce wave longs to attack the southern world, to battle against the wide sky and to listen to the music of the swans.

When the wind blows from the west over the sea of fierce currents, it longs to go eastward past us to capture the sun-tree in the wide, far-distant sea.

When the wind sets from the south over the land of the Saxons of stout shields and strikes the wave of Skiddy Island, it surges up to the top of Calad Nit [Kenmare Head?] *with a leafy, blue-grey cloak.*

The ocean is full, the sea in flood; beautiful is the palace of the ships; the sandy wind has thrown eddies round Inber na Da Ainmech; the rudder goes swift in the wide sea.

Sleep is uneasy, a rude, violent omen, with crushing triumph and stormy battle. The pallor of the swan has covered the plain of whales and its inhabitants; the hair of Manannán's wife blows loose.

The flood with its great force has burst over every broad river-mouth. The wind has come to us, winter's fury has killed us. Round Cantyre, round the land of Scotland, rushes a wild torrent, mountainous and fearful.

Son of God the Father with mighty hosts, save me from the horror of rough storms. Pure Master of the Sacrament, protect me from the great blast, from Hell with its furious tempest.

¶ Edited from the unique MS. Laud 610, fo. 10a, by Kuno Meyer, *Otia Merseiana*, II, 76–83.

30

THE ONLY JEALOUSY OF EMER

This dramatic scene is from the romance called 'The Sick-bed of Cú Chulainn'. As poets of the tenth and eleventh centuries imitated archaic metres, this story-teller seems to be imitating an archaic form, such as we find in the older sagas.

In another late version of a saga called 'Bricriu's Feast' the same writer appears to have composed 'The Logomachy of the Ulster Women', a dramatic scene that is less successful than the one printed here.

Cú Chulainn:
    (*to Loeg*) Fég, a Loíg, dar th'éis!
        Oc coistecht frit filet mná cóiri cíallmaithi
        co scenaib glasgéraib ina ndeslámaib,
        co n-ór fria n-uchtbruinnib.
        Cruth caín at-chíchiter
        amal tacait láith gaile dar cathchairptiu.
        Glé ro soí gné Emer ingen Forgaill.

    (*to Fand*) Nít ágara, ocus nícon tora etir.
        Tairsiu isin creit cumachta
        lasin suidi ngríanda
        form dreichse fo-déin.
        Ar dot-esarcoinéb-siu ar andrib ilib imdaib
        i cetharaird Ulad,

>   ar cía nos báigea ingen Fhorgaill
>   a hucht a comalta in ngním co cumachta
>   bés ní lim lamathar.
>
> (*to Emer*)   Not sechnaim-se, a ben,
>   amal shechnas cách a chárait.
>   Ním rubai-se do gae crúaid crithlámach
>   ná do scían tím thanaide
>   ná t'fherg thréith thimaircthech,
>   ar is mórdoilig mo nert
>   do thascor co niurt mná.
>
> EMER: Ceist trá, cid fod-rúair latsu, a Chú Chu-
>   lainn,
>   mo dímíad-sa fíad aindrib ilib in chúicid
>   ocus fíad aindrib ilib na hÉrenn
>   ocus fíad aís einig ar-chena?
>   Ar is fót chlith tánac-sa
>   ocus fo ollbríg do thairisen,
>   ar cía not báigea úall ollimresan
>   bés nípad rith lat-su mo lécun-sa,
>   a gillai, cía no tríalltá.
>
> CÚ CHULAINN: Ceist trá, a Emer,
>   cid arná léicfideá dam-sa
>   mo denus i ndáil mná?
>   Ar chétus in bensa,
>   is sí in glan genmnaid
>   gel gasta dingbála
>   do ríg ilchrothach ind ingensin
>   do thonnaib dar leraib lánmoraib
>   co ndeilb ocus écosc ocus soerchenél,

co ndruini ocus lámda ocus lámthorud
co céill ocus chonn ocus chobsaidecht
co n-immad ech ocus bótháinte.
Ar ní fil fo nim
ní bad tol ria coimchéile
ná dingned cía no comgelltá.
A Emer, ní foigeba-su curaid caín créchtach
cathbúadach badam fíu-sa.

EMER: Bés nícon fherr in ben día lenai.
Acht chena is álainn cech nderg, is gel cach nua,
is caín cech n-ard, is serb cech ngnáth,
cáid cech n-écmais, is faill cech n-aichnid
co festar cech n-éolas.

CÚ CHULAINN: *Look behind you, Loeg! Honourable, sensible women are listening to you with sharp grey knives in their right hands and gold on their breasts. You will see a fine sight, as though they were firebrand warriors coming over warchariots. Clearly Emer, Forgall's daughter, has changed her character.*

Do not be afraid and she will not approach. Come and sit before me in the great chariot with the sun-bright seat. I shall protect you from all the many women in the four quarters of Ulster. For though Forgall's daughter in the midst of her company threaten a desperate deed, with me, perhaps, she will not dare.

I avoid you, O woman, as all things avoid their yoke. The hard spear in your trembling hand, and your weak thin dagger, and your timid feeble fury cannot wound me because it is impossible to defeat my strength with a woman's strength.

EMER: Tell me, Cú Chulainn, what caused you to make a show of me before all the girls of the province, and all the girls of Ireland, and all decent people? For I came under your protection, and the main power of your guarantee, and though now you may boast in the pride of your conquest, perhaps even yet you will not succeed in abandoning me, my lad, though you try.

CÚ CHULAINN: And tell me, Emer, why will you not let me have my day of meeting with a woman? Because, to begin with, this woman is pure and chaste and bright and clever, a girl worthy of a victorious king from beyond the waves of mighty seas, with beauty and grace and good breeding. She knows embroidery and crafts and household skills. She has sense and wisdom and character, and many horses and herds of cattle, and there is nothing under heaven that she would not do that a noble husband desired of her if it were agreed on.

Ah, Emer, you will never find a handsome wound-dealing victorious warrior as good as I am.

EMER: And perhaps the woman you pursue is no better. But indeed everything red is beautiful, everything new is bright, everything unattainable is lovely, everything familiar is bitter, everything absent is perfect, everything known is neglected, until all knowledge is known.

¶ Edited by Myles Dillon from LU and H.4.22 in *Serglige Con Culainn* (Dublin, 1953).

31
WINTER

This is one of four poems, apparently written somewhere near Roscommon in the tenth or eleventh century, in various styles. It is one of the most brilliant poems in Irish, written in a style so simple and direct that, except for an odd word like *aicher*, 'bitter', it can be read as if it were Modern Irish, which is how we print it.

Fuit, fuit!
Fuar a-nocht Magh leathan Luirg;
   airde an sneachta ionás an sliabh,
   nocha roicheann fiadh a gcuid.

Fuit go bráth!
Ro dháil an doineann ar chách;
   abhann gach eitrighe a bhfán
   agus is linn lán gach áth.

Is muir mór gach loch bhíos lán
   agus is loch lán gach linn;
ní roichid eich tar Áth Rois,
   ní mó roichid dí chois inn.

Siubhladh ar iasc Inse Fáil;
   ní fhuil tráigh nach tiobrann tonn;
a mbroghaibh nocha tá broc,
   ní léir cloch, ní labhair corr.

WINTER

Ní fhagbhaid coin Choille Cuan
    sámh ná suan i n-adhbhaidh chon;
ní fhaghbhann an dre-án beag
    díon dá nead i Leitir Lon.

Is mairg do mheanbhaigh na n-éan
    an ghaoth ghéar is an t-oighreadh fuar;
ní fhaghbhann lon droma daoil
    díon a thaoibh i gCoilltibh Cuan.

Sádhail ar gcoire dá dhrol,
    aistreach lon ar Leitir Cró;
do mhínigh sneachta Coill Ché,
    deacair dréim ré Beanna Bó.

Cubhar Glinne Ridhe an fhraoigh
    ón ngaoith aichir do-gheibh léan;
mór a thruaighe agus a phian,
    an t-oighreadh do shiad 'na bhéal.

Éirghe do cholcaidh is do chlúimh —
    tug dot úidh! — nochan ciall duit;
iomad n-oighridh ar gach n-áth
    is é fáth fá n-abraim 'Fuit!'

    Brr! Brr! Wide Moylurg is cold tonight; the snow is higher than the hill, the deer cannot reach their food.
    Brr! Hell's bells! The storm has spread over everything. Every downhill channel is a river and every ford a flooded lake.
    Every full lake is a sea and every pool a full lake. Horses cannot reach across Ross Ford, and no more can two feet reach it.

The fish of Ireland are in motion. There is no strand the wave does not pound. There is no badger in the lands; no stony path is clear, no crane talks.

The wolves of Cuan Wood get no rest or repose in their lairs; the little wren does not find shelter for his nest in Leitir Lon.

Pity the young of the birds with the sharp wind and the cold ice! The blackbird with the beetle-dark back finds no shelter for his side in Cuan Wood.

Restful is our pot on its hook, but storm-tossed is the blackbird of Leitir Cró. Snow has smoothed Key Wood; it is hard to climb up Benbo.

The eagle of heathery Glen Rye suffers from the bitter wind. Great is his suffering and pain; the ice blows into his mouth.

To get up from quilt and feathers — mind what I say — is no sense for you. There is a lot of ice on every ford — that is why I say 'Brr!'

¶ Edited from the unique BM Harleian MS. 5280, fo. 35a, by Kuno Meyer, *RC*, XI, 130–4.

32

SUMMER

From the same — apparently Roscommon — group comes this extraordinarily ingenious little poem, which is the last word in wit and sophistication. All the verses but the fifth and last are in a five-syllable metre with three strong beats at the end of each line, and can be sung to the tune of 'The White Cockade'; the others are in a six-syllable metre that resembles a waltz. Translated into English it always sounds like something from the Japanese, but it is really more like Gilbert and Sullivan on one of their best days.

    Tánic sam slán sóer
      dia mbí clóen caill chíar;
    lingid ag seng snéid
      dia mbí réid rón rían.

    Canaid cuí ceól mbláith
      dia mbí súan sáim réid;
    lengait eóin ciúin crúaich
      ocus daim lúaith léith.

    Foss n-oss ro gab tess,
      gairid dess cass cúan,
    tibid trácht find fonn
      diambi lonn ler lúath.

Fúam ngáeth mbáeth i mbruig
    dairi duib Druim Daill;
rethid graig máel múad
    dia mbí dín Cúan Caill.

Maidid glass for cach lus,
    bilech doss daire glais;
tánic sam, ro fáith gam,
    goinit dam cuilinn chais.

Canaid lon dron dord
    diambi forbb caill cherb;
Súanaid ler lonn líach,
    fo-ling íach brec bedc.

Tibid grían dar cach tír —
    dedlaid lim fri sín sal —
garit coin, dáilit daim,
    forbrit brain, tánic sam!

Summer's come, healthy free, that bows down the dark wood; the slim, spry deer jumps and the seal's path is smooth.

The cuckoo sings sweet music, and there is smooth, soft sleep. Birds skim the quiet hill and the swift grey stags.

The deer's lair is too hot, and active packs cry pleasantly; the white stretch of strand smiles and the swift sea grows rough.

There is a noise of wanton winds in the palace of the oakwood of Drumdell; the fine clipped horses who shelter in Cuan Wood are rushing about.

Green bursts out from every plant; leafy is the shoot of the green oakwood. Summer has come, winter gone, twisted hollies hurt the stag.

The hardy blackbird who owns the thorny wood sings a bass; the wild, weary sea reposes and the speckled salmon leaps.

Over every land the sun smiles for me a parting greeting to bad weather. Hounds bark, stags gather, ravens flourish, summer's come!

¶ Printed by Kuno Meyer from the unique MS. (see Rawlinson, MS. B.502, facs. 106) in *Four Old Irish Songs of Summer and Winter* (London, 1903).

33

THE FOUR SEASONS

Two groups of poems in unrhymed metres, one of them on the best time for travelling, the other on the best animal for meat, are strung together in a thin eleventh-century tale with which they seem to have little to do. They may well be textbook pieces intended to illustrate for students the technique of archaic Irish verse. The lines are linked by chain alliteration, two words in each line alliterating with the first stressed word in the succeeding line, somewhat like this:

> Fall is no man's travelling time;
> Tasks are heavy; husbandmen
> Heed the low light. . . .

None of the three manuscripts in which these poems are preserved gives us a text with full alliteration; since we believe that this ornament was an integral part of the metre we have attempted to restore it.

1. *Autumn*

> Ráithe fó foiss fogamar,
> feidm and for ech oenduini
> fri oíb na llá lángairit.
> Loíg brecca i ndiaid deisseilte,
> dínit rúadgaiss raithnige.
> Rethait daim a dumachaib
> fri dordán na damgaire.

Dercain, subai i síthchailltib,
slatta etha imm ithgurtu
  ós íath domuin duinn.
Draigin, drissi delgnacha
fri duai in láir lethshlissi,
lán do mess tromm teinnithir,
do-tuittet cnoí cainmessa
  cuill, robili ráth.

2. *Winter*

Dubu ráithib rogemred;
robarta tonn túargabar
  iar toíb betha blaí.
Brónach cach én íathmaige
acht fíach fola fordeirge
  fri fúaimm gemrid gairg.
Gaim dub dorcha dethaite —
díumassaig coin chnámchomaig;
cuirthir ar aed íarnlestar
  iar ló dorcha dub.

3. *Spring*

Glass úar errach aigide;
úacht ina gaíth gignither,
glaedait lachain linnuisci,
luinnécnach corr cruadéigme
cluinit daim a ndíthrebaib
fri dúsacht moch matanraid.
Medraid eónu a hinnsénaib,
imda fíad ré fírtheichit
  a fid, a feór glass.

4. *Summer*

Fó sín samrad síthaister,
sám fid forard forglide
    nach fet gaíthe glúaiss;
Glass clúm caille clithaige,
cerba srotha saebuisci,
    sén i fótán fó.

1. Autumn is an excellent season for staying at home; there is a load for everyone's horse in the harvest of the shortening days. Dappled fawns drop in the wake of hinds, nurslings of the red stalk of the heather. Stags run from dunes at the clamour of the herd. There are acorns and berries in peaceful woodlands, and cornstalks round cornfields over the range of the brown earth. There are thorns and spiky brambles by the rampart of the house site with the broken wall. The hard earth is full of heavy fruit. Nuts fall, the good fruits of the hazel, the great tree of forts.

2. Deep winter is the blackest of seasons, a storm of waves is raised against the border of the earth's lands. Every bird of the plain is sorrowful at the roar of rude winter except the red and bloody raven. Winter, black, dark and smoky! Bone-chewing dogs are arrogant; the iron pot is put on the fire at the end of the dark, black day.

3. Bitter-cold is icy spring; cold will be born in its wind. The ducks freeze to the pond. Wild and mournful is the crane of the harsh cry that the stags hear in their wildernesses at the early start of morning. It wakes the birds from islands; many are the wild animals from which they flee out of the wood, out of the green grass.

4. Summer is a fine season for long journeys. Calm is the high, choice wood that no breath of wind stirs. Green is the plumage of the sheltering wood, streams of wandering water are dried up, there is a good omen in the fine turf.

¶ The reading of the three MSS. are printed in *Ériu*, VII, 2-4 and 197-8.

34
A PRAYER
FOR RECOLLECTION

As Middle Irish religious poetry becomes metrically tidier it tends to lose both freshness and range; this poem is remarkable because it is exceedingly neat but preserves both. Meyer, who first published it, placed it in the tenth century, but it seems later.

Is mebul dom imrádud
  a méit élas úaim;
ad-águr a imgábud
  i lló brátha búain.

Tresna salmu sétaigid
  for conair nád cóir,
reithid, búaidrid, bétaigid,
  fiad roscaib Dé móir.

Tre airechta athlama,
  tre buidne ban mboeth,
tre choillte, tre chathracha,
  is lúaithiu ná in goeth.

Tresna sétu sochraide
  ind ala fecht dó,

tre dimbíthe dochraide
fecht aile, ní gó.

Cen ethar 'na chloenchéimmim
    cingid tar cach ler;
lúath linges 'na oenléimmim
    ó thalmain co nem.

Reithid, ní rith rogaíse,
    i n-ocus, i céin;
iar réimmenaib robaíse
    taidlid dia thig féin.

Ce thrialltar a chuimrech-som
    nó geimel 'na chois,
ní cunnail, ní cuimnech-som
    co ngabad feidm fois.

Foebur ná fúaimm flescbuille
    ní traethat co tailc;
sleimnithir eirr n-escuinge
    oc dul as mo glaicc.

Glas, nó charcar chromdaingen,
    nó chuimrech for bith,
dún, nó ler, nó lomdaingen
    nín astat dia rith.

Taet, a Chríst choím chertgenmnaid,
    dianid réil cech rosc,
rath in Spirta sechtdelbaig
    dia choimét, dia chosc.

> Follamnaig mo chride-se,
>   a Dé dúilig déin,
>   corop tú mo dile-se,
>   co ndernar do réir.

> Rís, a Chríst, do chétchummaid,
>   ro bem imma-lle;
>   níta anbsaid éccunnail
>   ní inonn is mé.

God help my thought, it strays from me so much! I fear danger from it on the day of eternal judgement.

Throughout the Psalms it travels a wrong road; it rushes, it shouts, it quarrels before the eyes of the great God.

Through thrusting throngs, through troops of lustful women, through woods, through cities, it is faster than the wind.

At one time along pleasant paths, at the next through rough, harsh ways — it is no lie.

In its crooked course it crosses every sea without a ferry; in one bound it leaps swiftly from earth to heaven.

It runs unwisely near and far; after depraved excursions it comes home.

Though one try to bind it or fetter its feet, it still is not constant, or mindful to take a spell of rest.

Neither sword nor hiss of the lash keeps it down completely; it is as slippery as an eel's tail dodging my grip.

Lock, nor harsh prison, nor chain on earth, fortress nor sea, nor grim castle holds it from its race.

Dear, most chaste Christ, to whom every eye is clear, may the grace of the sevenfold spirit come to keep it, control it.

Govern my heart, stern God of the elements, and be my love and let me do your will.

May I be one of your chosen company; may we be together; you are not unstable or infirm — unlike me.

¶ See Kuno Meyer, *Ériu*, III, 13 ff., and *EIL*, 38 ff.

35

THE HERMITAGE

This lovely little poem, which Gerard Murphy would place in the tenth century, has the pure singing note of early Irish poetry. It is attributed to St. Manchán, after whom Lemanaghan in Offaly is named, but this merely means that it was incorporated into a saint's 'Life'.

> Dúthracar, a Maic Dé bí,
>   a Rí suthain sen,
> bothán deirrit díthreba
>   commad sí mo threb.
>
> Uisce treglas tanaide
>   do buith ina taíb,
> linn glan do nigi phectha
>   tría rath Spirta Naíb.
>
> Fidbaid álainn immocus
>   impe do cech leith
> fri haltrom n-én n-ilgothach
>   fri clithar dia cleith.
>
> Deisebar fri tesugud,
>   sruthán dar a lainn,
> talam togu co méit raith
>   bad maith do cach clainn.

THE HERMITAGE

Úathad óclach n-innide —
 in-fessam a llín —
ot é umlai urluithi
 d'urguidi ind Ríg.

Ceithri triir, trí cethrair,
 cuibdi fri cach les;
dá sheiser i n-eclais
 eter túaid is tes.

Sé desa do imfhorcraid
 immumsa fo-déin
co guidi tre bithu sír
 ind Ríg ruithes gréin.

Eclais aíbinn anartach,
 aitreb Dé do nim,
sutralla soillsi íar sain
 úas scriptúir glain gil.

Oentegdais do aithigid
 fri deithidin cuirp,
cen drúis, cen intládud,
 cen imrádud n-uilc.

Is é trebad no gébainn,
 do-gegainn cen chleith:
fírchainnen chumra, cerca,
 bratáin breca, beich.

Mo lórtu brait ocus bíd
 ónd Ríg as chaín clú,
mo buithsi im shuidi fri ré
 oc guidi Dé i nach dú.

O Son of the living God, old eternal King, I desire a hidden hut in the wilderness that it may be my home.

A narrow little blue stream beside it and a clear pool for the washing away of sin through the grace of the Holy Ghost.

A lovely wood close about it on every side, to nurse birds with all sorts of voices and to hide them with its shelter.

Looking south for heat, and a stream through its land, and good fertile soil suitable for all plants.

A number of virtuous youths — I shall tell their number — humble and obedient to beseech the King.

Four threes, three fours, suitable for all good service; two sixes in the church, one north one south.

Six pairs beside myself praying for ever to the King who moves the sun.

A beautiful draped church, a home for God from Heaven, and bright lights above the clean white Gospels.

One household to visit for care of the body, without lust or weakness or thought of evil.

The husbandry I would do and choose without concealment is fragrant fresh leeks and hens and speckled salmon and bees.

Enough of clothing and food from the King of fair fame, and to be sitting for a while and praying God in every place.

¶ Printed from the unique MS. 23.N.10, by Kuno Meyer, *Ériu*, 1, 39.

36

THE PILGRIM

    Kuno Meyer took the author of this poem to be Cormac mac Cuileannáin, the scholarly King of Munster who was killed at Balagh Moon in 903, but it is later than his time. As it stands, not only is the text incomplete, but a great many new verses have been added to it; these we have omitted.

    In regsa, a Rí inna rún,
       íar coimse clúm ocus céol,
    mo brogad for mara múr
       mo chúl do thochar frim éol?

    In mbia i mbochtai isin chath
       tre rath in Ríg, rí cen meth,
    cen míad mór, cen charpat cloth,
       cen ór, cen argat, cen ech?

    Cen ól medrach mesctha druing,
       cen túaith truim, cen teglach torm,
    cen brasscíath, cen aile n-arm,
       cen chúach, cen chuirm is cen chorn?

    Cen éitiud mín mass ar súil,
       cen chlúim nád cara nach naíb,
    acht barrán beithe fo búaid
       fo chuilche chrúaid frim dá thaíb?

In timgér celebrad cóir
   d'innsi móir macc Míled múaid?
Indom tairber fo Chríst cuing
   ria techt tar tuinn Mara Ruaid?

In ráidiubsa, rád ndíuit ndían,
   mo choibsen cían, comol crúaid?
In ferfat, a Rí na néll,
   frassa mo dér tar mo grúaid?

In tiurr mo láim do cach crécht
   for brú tuinne tinnbi bárc?
In fuicéb oc mara múr
   slicht mo da glún isin trácht?

In toicéb mo churchán cíar
   ós oicén uchtlethan án?
In reg, a Rí ríchid réil
   as mo thoil féin for in sál?

Imba sessach, imba seng,
   imba tressach tuirme glonn,
a Chríst, in cuingéna frimm,
   ó thí co techt tar linn lonn?

Shall I go, O King of the Mysteries, after my fill of cushions and music, to turn my face on the shore and my back on my native land?

Shall I be in poverty in the battle through the grace of the King, a King who does not fail, without great honour or a famous chariot, without silver and without a horse?

Without heady drink that intoxicates a throng, without a stout tribe, without retainers to protect me, without a swift shield or any weapon, without cup, ale, or drinking-horn?

Without soft clothes that are pleasant to look at, without cushions, which are no friend of any saint, but beech-twigs of virtue under a hard quilt for my body?

Shall I say a long farewell to the great island of the sons of proud Míl? Shall I offer myself under Christ's yoke before I cross the waters of the Red Sea?

Shall I make my long confession, swiftly and simply, on this hard occasion? Shall I, O King of the Clouds, shed showers of tears over my cheek?

Shall I cut my hand with every sort of wound on the breast of the wave which wrecks boats? Shall I leave the track of my two knees on the strand by the shore?

Shall I take my little black curragh over the broad-breasted, glorious ocean? O King of the bright kingdom, shall I go of my own choice upon the sea?

Whether I be strong or poor, or mettlesome so as to be recounted in tales, O Christ, will you help me when it comes to going upon the wild sea?

¶ Printed from the unique MS. 23.N.10, by Kuno Meyer, ZCP, x, 45–47.

37

FELLOW FEELING

A good example of the later lyric poetry. It is impossible to be sure of the date, but it probably belongs to the twelfth century. We have followed the example of previous editors by giving it in modern spelling.

Cumhthach labhras an lonsa,
an t-olc do fhuair d'fheadarsa;
   cidh bé do théalaigh a theagh
   is fá éanaibh do hairgeadh.

An t-olc fhuairsean a-nossa
ní cian uaidh ó fhuarassa,
   maith m'aithne ar do labhra, a luin,
   a haithle th'adhbha d'argain.

Do chridhese, a luin, do loisc
a ndearna an duine díchoisc —
   do nead gan éan is gan uigh,
   sgéal is beag ar an mbuachail.

Tigdís fád ghothaibh glana
do muinntir nua a-nallana;
   éan nocha dtig as do thaigh
   tar béal do nid ba neanaidh.

Do mharbhsad buach aille bó
do chlannsa uile i n-aonló;
 ionann sódh damhsa agus duit
 mo chlannsa ní mó maraid.

Do bhí ag ingheilt go hadhaigh
leithéan an eóin allmharaigh,
 do-chuaidh ar an sás iar sin
 go bhfuair bás leisin mbuachail.

A Fhir do chum an cruinne
doiligh linn do leatruime;
 na caraid atá rér dtaoibh
 maraid a mná is a macaoimh.

Táinig sluagh sídh 'na sidhe
do mharbhadh ar muintire;
 gion go ró gádh mé ón ghuin
 nocha mó ár ó armaibh.

Cumha ar mná, cumha ar gclainne
tréan a imshníomh orainne;
 gan a slighe a-muigh 's a-mach
 do thuil mo chridhe cumhthach.

It is sadly the blackbird calls; I know the wrong that has been done him. The one who wrecked his house has destroyed his fledgelings.
The wrong that has been done to him now was recently done to me; well I recognize your call, blackbird, after the destruction of your house.

What the violent man did, blackbird, has scalded your heart; the cowherd cares little that there is neither fledgeling nor eggs in your house.

Your newly born children used to come at your clear call; now no fledgeling comes out of your house, nettles have grown over the mouth of your nest.

The cowherds killed all your children in one day; your fate was the same as mine — my children live no longer.

The mate of the bird from across the sea was feeding until nightfall; she went into the trap after that and was killed by the cowherd.

O Man who made the world, I resent Thy partiality; the wives and children of the friends around me are still alive.

A fearful host came like a blast to kill my people; although I am not in danger of being killed myself, death by weapons is no worse.

Sorrow for my wife and children is a strong torment to me; that they no longer go in and out has filled my sorrowful heart.

¶ Published from the unique MS. LB, 186, by Kuno Meyer, *GJ*, IV, 42, and *ISP*, 29.

38

EVE

The one thing that Irish poets did not do was to write dramatic lyrics in the air, in the manner of Browning. Consequently the reason for this incisive, brilliant little poem is something of a mystery, unless it comes from some romance about the Biblical story of creation, of the kind we have already seen exemplified in *Saltair na Rann*.

> Mé Eba, ben Ádaim uill;
>   mé ro sháraig Ísu thall;
> mé ro thall nem ar mo chloinn;
>   cóir is mé do-chóid sa crann.
>
> Ropa lem ríched dom réir,
>   olc in míthoga rom thár;
> olc in cosc cinad rom chrín;
>   fo-rír, ní hidan mo lám.
>
> Mé tuc in n-uball an-úas
>   do-chúaid tar cumang mo chraís;
> in céin marat sain re lá,
>   de ní scarat mná re baís.
>
> Ní bíad eigred in cach dú,
>   ní bíad geimred gaethmar glé,
> ní bíad iffern, ní bíad brón,
>   ní bíad oman, minbad mé.

I am Eve, the wife of noble Adam; it was I who violated Jesus in the past; it was I who robbed my children of heaven; it is I by right who should have been crucified.

I had heaven at my command; evil the bad choice that shamed me; evil the punishment for my crime that has aged me; alas, my hand is not pure.

It was I who plucked the apple; it went past the narrow of my gullet; as long as they live in daylight women will not cease from folly on account of that.

There would be no ice in any place; there would be no bright windy winter; there would be no hell, there would be no grief, there would be no terror but for me.

¶ Published from B. IV. 2 by Kuno Meyer, *Ériu*, III, 148; for some further readings from British Museum Add. MS. 19995, see *EIL*, 51.

39

THE SCRIBE

The eleventh-century revival of the cult of St. Colum Cille by the Ulster clerics resulted in the attribution of hundreds of contemporary poems to him. Sometimes the ascription is guileless as here; sometimes, as in no. 40, a verse or two was added by a pious forger.

> Is scíth mo chrob ón scríbainn;
> ní dígainn mo glés géroll;
> sceithid penn — gulban caelda —
> dig ndaelda do dub g¹égorm.
>
> Bruinnid srúaim n-ecna ndedairn
> as mo láim degduinn desmais;
> doirtid a dig for duilinn
> do dub in chuilinn chnesglais.
>
> Sínim mo phenn mbec mbraenach
> tar aenach lebar lígoll
> cen scor fri selba ségonn,
> dían scíth mo chrob ón scríbonn.

My hand is tired from writing; my sharp pen is not steady; the pen, a slender beak, spouts a dark stream of blue ink. An unceasing stream of wisdom pours from my brown, shapely hand; it spills its flow of ink from the blue-skinned holly over the page.

I send my wet little pen over a whole fair of lovely books without ceasing for the wealth of great ones, and so my hand is tired from writing.

¶ Published from the unique MS. by Kuno Meyer, *ZCP*, XIII, 8. The emendation of *ndefhinn* to *ndedairn* in line 5 is that of Gerard Murphy.

40

FAITH

There are two independent recensions of this poem, the first, which we give here, eleventh or twelfth century, and the other later; from both it is perfectly clear that we are dealing not with one poem, but with several. Obviously the original, whatever it may have been like, was so popular that people revised it, added to it, and forgot what it was all about. Even in the better of the two recensions, edited by Professor Carney, there are different layers of language, metre, and poetic talent.

M'aenarán dam isa slíab,
  a Rí rían, rop soraid sét;
ním nessa éc ina beinn
  indás no beinn tríchait cét.

Cia no beinn tríchait cét
  don ócbaid tét, tenna a cnis,
dia tí caingen in báis brais
  ní fhil daingen gabas fris.

Ní fhil innil i nach dú
do mac duine acht rop trú;
  ní chuala nech dia mbad toich
  belach fors ngondais étroich.

Cia dúthraiged nech mo brath,
cid santach im scripulrad,
  nó corop deóin Fíadat finn,
  cia imráidi, ní cumaing.

Ní cumaing duinén a-niú
mo shaegul do thimdibiu
  acht in Rí ro delb in sam
  Coimdiu nime ocus talman.

Ním derbann do dul for fecht
cia shréidid nech i n-airecht;
  fót fors ndelbad mo lecht
  issum écen a thairecht.

In laech renas a chnes mbán
  isin áth fri galar ngúr,
ní nessa dó éc, cid baeth,
  indás don gaeth bís ar cúl.

Cia dú do fhir chonaire
  cuingid comairce for sét?
isin chomairce do-thét
  caide a chomairce ar éc?

Aminecán, cia thora
do neoch imgabáil gona,
  tairic a laethe baeguil
  do chách i cinn a shaeguil.

> For faesam Dé úasail áin,
> Athair naí ngrád, spirit naem,
> ním reilci i n-úathaib báis báin,
> a ngráin cia nom tegma im aen.

When I go alone into the mountain, O King of Roads, may it be a fortunate journey. Death is no nearer to me on its peak than if I were guarded by thirty hundred men.

Even if I had thirty hundred hot youths with stout skins, when the call of swift death comes there is no fortress that holds out against it.

There is no snare in any place for the son of man unless he be doomed. Nobody, even if he wished it, has heard of a road on which those not doomed could be killed.

Though anyone should try to encompass me, though he were jealous of my goods, though he may meditate it he cannot achieve it until the fair Lord will it.

No little human being today can shorten my life, but only the King who shaped the summer, the Lord of Heaven and earth.

That someone should sneeze in the assembly does not stop me from setting out on a journey; I must come to the piece of earth for which my tomb has been ordained.

The warrior who barters his white flesh in the ford for bitter injury — he may be foolish, but death is no nearer him than to the wise man who stays behind.

What use is it to the traveller to seek company on his journey? In the company that goes, what is his protection against death?

So be it! Though a man may avoid death, his day of danger comes to everyone at the end of his life.

Under the protection of the noble, splendid God, the Father of nine orders, the Holy Ghost, let Him not leave me in the terrors of white death, though their horror come to me when I am alone.

¶ Edited by James Carney, from NLI.G.3 and H.3.18, in *Éigse*, II, 107–13.

41

HYMN TO ST. MICHAEL

Mael Ísu Ó Brolchán, who died on pilgrimage in Lismore in the year 1086, was the most famous religious poet of his time.

A aingil,
   beir, a Michil mórfhertaig,
cosin Coimdid mo chaingin.

In cluini?
   Cuinnig co Día ndílgudach
dílgud m'uilc adbail uili.

Ná fuirig!
   Beir mo dúthracht ndiúpartach
cosin Ríg, cosin Ruirig.

Dom anmain
   tuc cobair, tuc comdídnad
i n-úair techta don talmain.

Co daingen
   ar chenn m'anma ernaides
tair co n-ilmílib aingel.

A mílid!
   For bith cam claen cosnamach
tair dom chobair da-rírib.

Ní tarda
 dínsium for a n-apraimsi,
i céin mairer ním fargba!

Not togaim
 cora saera m'anmainsi,
mo chonn, mo chéill, mo cholainn.

A chaingnig,
 a choscaraig cathbúadaig,
a marbaid Anchríst ainglig.

Angel! Great-miracled Michael, carry my request to the Lord.
Do you hear me? Ask of the forgiving God forgiveness for all my great evil.
Do not delay! Carry my greedy request to the King, to the High King.
Bring help, bring protection to my soul in its hour of leaving earth.
To meet my waiting soul come stoutly with many thousands of angels.
Warrior, against the crooked, twisted, warring world come to my help indeed.
Do not spurn what I say, do not desert me while I live!
I choose you to redeem my mind, my sense, my body.
Intercessor, victorious fighter, angelic slayer of Antichrist!

¶ Edited from H.2.16 and Laud 610 by Kuno Mayer in *Cath Finntrága* (Oxford, 1885), 88–89.

42

MAEL ÍSU FINDS HIS PSALTER AGAIN

In publishing this exquisite poem, Meyer suggested that it was probably addressed to one of the *virgines subintroductae*, the pious women who in early times kept house for clerics, and it was James Carney who pointed out that it was really addressed to a Psalm-book, lost, then rediscovered in old age. What gives the poem its magic is that it begins in the language of courtly love and then mounts to a great crescendo of religious passion.

Professor Carney is also probably right when he attributes this to Mael Ísu Ó Brolchán, but it should be said that nothing else of Mael Ísu's has the same quality.

> A Chrínóc, cubaid do cheól,
>   cencobat fíróc, at fíal;
> ro mósam túaid i tír Néill
>   tan do-rónsam feis réid ríam.

> Rop sí m'aes tan ro fóis lem,
>   a bé níata in gaesa grinn,
> daltán clíabglan caem nád cam,
>   maccán mall secht mblíadan mbinn.

> Bámar for bith Banba bailc
>   cen éilniud anma ná cuirp,

mo lí lasrach lán dot sheirc
    amal geilt cen aslach uilc.

Erlam do chomairle chóir,
    dóig nos togamne in cech tír,
is ferr rográd dod gaeis géir
    ar comrád réid risin Ríg.

Ro fóis re cethrar íar sin
    im díaid, cen nach methlad mer,
ro-fetar, is beóda in blad,
    at glan cen pheccad re fer.

Fo deóid dom-rúachtais a-rís
    íar cúartaib scís, gleó co ngaeis,
do-dechaid temel tart gnúis,
    cen drúis is dered dot aeis.

At inmain lemsa cen locht;
    rot bía mo chensa cen chacht;
ní léicfe ar mbádud i péin
    fo-gabam crábud léir latt.

Lán dod labra in bith búan,
    adbal do rith tar cach rían,
dia seichmis cech día do dán
    ro-seismis slán co Día ndían.

Do-beire do thimna toí
    do chách co imda ar bith ché;
síthlai dúin uile in cech ló
    ní gó guide díchra Dé.

MAEL ÍSU FINDS HIS PSALTER AGAIN

Do-rata Día Debraid dúin
ar ré rit ar menmain mín;
rop rolainn rinn gnúis Ríg réil
íar n-ar léim ór colainn chrín.

Crionóg, it is proper to sing of you; even though you are no longer young, you are chaste. We grew up in the north, in Ulster, at the time when we slept sweetly together.

When you slept with me, valiant maiden of the sharp wisdom, I was a pure-hearted, quiet, uncomplicated lad, a gentle boy of seven sweet years.

We travelled the great world of Ireland without soiling of soul or body, my burning eye full of love for you, like a madman still untempted by evil.

Your good advice is ever prompt — no wonder I chose it in every land; great love for your keen wisdom is better if we would talk easily with the King.

You slept with four men after that, when you had left me, with no foolish weakness; I know, for it is famous, that you are free from sin with any man.

At last you have reached me again after weary journeys — a shrewd conflict; your face has darkened, the end of your life is without lust.

I love you blamelessly; you will have welcome from me without stint. You will not let me drown in hell — I find true piety with you.

The lasting world is full of your fame; marvellous is your travelling on every road. If I followed your teaching every day I should safely reach stern God.

You give your silent testimony to all men on earth, and expound to us daily that it is no lie to pray God earnestly.

May the God of Judgement grant to me to spend my remaining time with you in peace of mind; may the face of the King of Heaven shine brightly for me when I escape from this withered body.

¶ For Kuno Meyer's editions, see *ZCP*, VI, 266, and *Sitzungsberichte* of the Prussian Academy, Phil.-Hist. Class (1918), 362 ff.; for James Carney's comments, see *Éigse*, IV, 280 ff.

43

GRACE BEFORE DEATH

Professor Carney seems fully justified in his attribution of this poem to Mael Ísu. It would be a coincidence if two Ulster poets both died in Munster at about the same time.

It is a curiously painful poem; the generalized piety and the individual suffering do not really blend, and one wishes that one or the other were allowed to dominate.

> At-lochar duit, a mo Rí
>   do-gní ar sochar ar bith cé;
> ó dom-rala i llige leóin
>   sé mís fo-deóid cus indé.
>
> A-tú mar chimmid i cipp
>   do tharrachtain immid uilc;
> súas beires m'anmain a-nocht
>   mo chorp isin talmain tuit.
>
> Dom-ratad i slabraid sunn,
>   maith don anmain as cach am;
> bec mo nert, am scíth bun 's cinn,
>   indar limm fom-fríth co fann.
>
> Ferr lemm, a degmaicc Dé déin,
>   cid léir in treblait rom thráig,
> iná fledól im thír thúaid
>   nó degór cen lúaig fom láim.

I llóg mo chuil is mo chelg
   mad rom gab muin, mó cech mairg;
dom-áraill, ní dúairc in t-ord,
   béim nád borb dot abainn aird.

A-túsa mar bís dall dub
   is mo thaeb co fann re fraig;
mon-úarachán, a Dé dil,
   mise trúagachán im thaig.

Testa mo nert, núall cen chleith,
   a Athair na slúag, nom saich!
Rom láis i cuimrech i cruich
   i-muich i tír Muimnech maith.

Ma tát co méit teimil truim
   mo dá rosc i ngeimil grinn,
ad-saílim, a Rí na rann,
   beithir tall co haíbinn inn.

Is é mo samail acht bec
   mar bís luch gabail ar gruic
ica crothad fo chrub chait,
   ní nád ait at-lochar duit.

Uch, nocha n-éirgim chen chneit,
   nocha téigim fo guth cluic,
ní gairit m'othar ar m'olc,
   a Dé, a-nocht at-lochar duit.

I give thanks to you, my King, who looks after our welfare in this world; it is six months from yesterday that I have been lying on my sick-bed.

I am like a prisoner in chains, visited by many evils; it carries my soul upward tonight, but my body sinks into the earth.

I have been thrown into fetters, which is good for my soul at any time. My strength is low, I am weak in head and foot; I may say that I am feeble indeed.

Good son of the stern God, though the troubles that afflict me are hard, I prefer them to a drinking-party in my own northern country or pure, and gold freely in my hand.

It is the worst of all troubles that if I have been tricked it is in payment for my sin and treachery; a gentle blow of your heavenly lash has caught me, a joyful judgement.

I am like a stone-blind man with my body turned weakly to the wall. My grief, dear God, I am only a poor victim in my own house.

My strength is gone, I cry it openly — Father of Hosts, come to me! You have chained me on a cross far away in the good land of the Munstermen.

If my eyes are bitterly locked in heavy clouds, I expect, King of songs, that on the other side I shall profit by it.

I am hardly better than a mouse, caught in a pronged trap and shaken in a cat's claw — I thank you for what is not a pleasure.

Ah! I can scarcely rise without a groan, or go when the bell calls. My illness does not approach my sins — God, I thank you this night.

¶ Edited by Kuno Meyer in the *Sitzungsberichte* of the Prussian Academy, Phil.-Hist. Class (1918), 371-4.

44
THE LAMENT FOR FER DIAD

The author of 'The Death of Fer Diad' in 'The Cattle Raid of Cooley' was no story-teller, God knows, but he was an interesting metrist. Cú Chulainn's lament for his friend is an excellent example of his skill, but the copyists have played the deuce with it. It is hard to say whether the first two lines, which are used as a chorus, are intended to be of six or seven syllables. Seven would be more effective, and perhaps we should read *Cluiche cách, uch, caíne cách*. The remaining lines are certainly intended to be of five syllables, and we have accordingly reduced them to this, though in the final verse it involves complete rewriting.

>Cluiche cách, caíne cách
>go roich Fer nDíad issin áth;
>inann foglaim dún
>inann rograim ráth,
>inann muimme maeth
>ron sluinne sech cách.

>Cluiche cách, caíne cách
>go roich Fer nDíad issin áth;
>inann aister úath
>inann gaisced gnáth,
>Scáthach tuc dá scíath
>damsa is Fer Díad tráth.

Cluiche cách, caíne cách
go roich Fer nDíad issin áth;
   inmain úaitne óir
     ro fhuirmius ar áth,
   a tharbga na túath
   ba calma ná cách.

Cluiche cách, caíne cách
go roich Fer nDíad issin áth;
   indar limm Fer Díad
     ro bíad limm co bráth;
   indé ba móir slíab
   indiu is lugu scáth.

All was sport, all was pleasure till Fer Diad in the ford. One was our study, one our gifts, one the gentle nurse who named us before all.

All was sport, all was pleasure till Fer Diad in the ford. One was our fearful journey, one our usual arms — Scáthach gave two shields once to Fer Diad and myself.

All was sport, all was pleasure till Fer Diad in the ford. Beloved was the golden pillar I struck down at the ford, O bull of the tribes that was braver than all!

All was sport, all was pleasure till Fer Diad in the ford. I thought Fer Diad would be with me for ever; yesterday he was as great as a mountain, today he is less than a shade.

¶ Based on the text in *LL* (eds. R. I. Best, O. Bergin, and M. A. O'Brien; Dublin, 1954), lines 10997–11024.

45

THE SONG OF THE HEADS

The story of Cormac mac Cuileannáin, King of Munster, who was killed in the battle of Balagh Moon in 903, apparently made an extraordinary impression on the imagination of the literary men. To begin with, of course, he was one of themselves, a scholar. Besides, he was a bishop: the Cashel dynasty is peculiar in that it seems to have tried to combine secular and religious rule. According to legend he was married to Gormfhlaith, daughter of the High King, who later married Cearbhall, King of Leinster, and finally Niall Black-knee, King of Dublin; his divorce from her is explained by a twelfth-century poet on the grounds of his celibacy as a bishop. Gormfhlaith in turn became the heroine of a romance, and there is a group of rather fine poems in which she is supposed to lament the death of Niall, but these are late medieval and do not fall within the scope of the present volume.

This poem is a ballad from a romance about Cormac's death; it probably is twelfth century, and we have put it into Modern Irish spelling.

> Truaghán sin, a Rí na Ríogh,
>   a Rí fíréan fichtibh sluagh!
> Is eólchaire ná gach ceól
>   ceól na gceann i n-oidhche fhuair.
>
> A chinn Ghéagáin, druid i-le,
> go ndearnamois coinnircle,

mór an ní fá dtugsam láimh,
oirfideadh meic Cuileannáin.

Ar dtriúr bhráthar dúinn a-réir;
  maith ar láthar um an slúagh,
a-nocht gé táid ar trí gcinn
  ag oirfideadh go tim truagh.

Och, mon-uar!
Gé gearr ó Dhomhnach go Luan,
  is giorra bhíos Rí na néall
déanamh tréan go mba truagh.

Do-rad ubhall gach fir dún
  flaith do bhí ag fulang sluagh,
agus do naisc oirn dá dheóin
  go ndiongnamais ceól budh truagh. . . .

Ochán, ach!
Do thuit Cormac insan chath;
  ó theasta a shíol as an mbioth
maise ríogh Caisil ad-bath.

Cormac a Tulach na Ríogh
  do ba rí ar Mumhain muadh;
gach ní do fhuighill a bhéal
  do fhuiling gach tréan is gach truagh.

Maith do shuidhe dabhach mór,
  maith do dhluighe ralach ruadh,
maith do thabhairt laoch a léan,
  maith do dhéanamh tréan do thruagh.

Camhaoir so, coisgidh bhur gceól,
   mithigh díbh éisteacht, mo nuar!
Beiridh beannachtain a-nocht
   is éirghidh chum bhur gcorp dtruagh.

Alas, O King of Kings, righteous King with scores of hosts, sadder than any music is the music of the heads in the cold night.

Géagán's head, come here, let us join together; it is a great task we have accepted, to make music for Cuileannán's son.

We were three brothers last night; good was our strength in the host, though tonight our three heads are making weak mournful music.

Alas, though it is a short time from Sunday to Monday, it is shorter for the King of the clouds to make strong men weak.

The prince who was supporting the hosts gave each of us an apple and pledged us to make sad music.

Alas, alas, Cormac fell in the battle; since his seed is lacking from the world the glory of the King of Cashel has perished.

Cormac from the Mound of the Kings was king over noble Munster; everything his mouth expressed, every strong man and weak one suffered.

He was good at establishing great vats, good at cleaving red oaks, good at bringing heroes low, good at making weak men strong.

It is dawn! Cease your music! It is time for you to be still, alas! Say farewell tonight and go back to your sad bodies.

¶ Printed from two MSS., Brussels 2324–40 and 23.F.16, in J. Fraser, P. Grosjean, and J. G. O'Keeffe, *Irish Texts* (London, 1931–3), III, 8–10.

46

THE PITY OF NATURE—II

Pacifism was not invented by the Quakers; it is implicit in the whole story of the Ulster king, Suibne, who is supposed to have gone mad during the battle of Mag Rath in 639 and taken refuge in the woods. A version of this story was already current in the eighth or ninth century, and it links up with early Irish nature poetry. Apparently in revolt against the pagan tradition of verse, which required it to be composed indoors and in darkness, the Christian poets tended to identify Christ with nature, and this splendid poem sums up their feelings with heart-breaking power. It is late Middle Irish, and we have transposed it into a modern spelling.

>   Binne liom um na tonna,
>   m'adhbha a-nocht ciodhat cranna,
>   ná griog-gráig chlogáin chille
>   an chú do-ní cuach Banna. . . .
>
>   Amhail thuairgid na mná an líon —
>   is fíor gé nom chluintear-sa —
>   amhlaidh ro thuairgid san chath
>   for Maigh Rath mo mhuinntear-sa.
>
>   Ó Loch Diolair na haille
>   go Doire Coluim Chille,
>   nocha deabhaidh ro chuala
>   ó ealaibh buadha binne.

Dord daimh dhíthreibhe ós aille,
bhíos a Síodhmhuine Glinne,
nochan fhuil ceól ar talmhain
im anmain acht a bhinne.

A Chríost, a Chríost, rom chluine!
A Chríost, a Chríost gan bhine!
A Chríost, a Chríost rom chara!
Nárom scara réd bhinne!

Though my dwelling tonight is in the trees, sweeter to me across the waves than the noise of a church bell is the cooing of the cuckoo of the Bann. . . .

As women scutch flax — it is true though I say it — so were my people scutched in battle over Mag Rath.

From Loch Diolair of the cliff to Derry of Colum Cille it was not strife I heard from swans proud and majestic.

The bellowing of the lonely stag from the cliffs in Siodhmhuine Glens, there is no music on earth in my soul but its sweetness.

Christ, Christ hear me! Christ, Christ without sin! Christ, Christ love me! Do not sever me from your sweetness!

¶ From the edition of *Buile Shuibhne* by J. G. O'Keeffe (ITS, XII), 18.

47

COLUM CILLE IN EXILE

We began this anthology with a seventh-century hymn to Colum Cille, then the most popular of Irish saints. But at the Synod of Whitby in 664 Wilfrid taunted the Irish monks with the doubtful orthodoxy of their founder, and suddenly, as if by magic, the name of Colum Cille disappears from the literature and that of St. Patrick — up to this time practically ignored — takes its place. Then, during the reform movement of the eleventh and twelfth centuries, probably because of the prominence of Ulstermen in it, Colum Cille comes back in scores of undistinguished poems; one manuscript, called the 'Psalter of Colum Cille', contains 150 of them. But this Colum Cille is a highly sentimentalized figure, as witness the suggestion that his part in the battle of Cúl Dremne was responsible for his exile, a charge the seventh-century poet repudiates. The smooth elegance of the verse compared with the classical poise of the earlier poem suggests that the later poet had heard Colum Cille well spoken of, the earlier had known him or his friends.

> Robad mellach, a Meic Muire,
>   dingnaib rémenn
> ascnam tar tuinn topur ndílenn
>   dochum nÉirenn.
>
> Co Mag nEólairg sech Beinn Foibne
>   tar Loch Febail,
> airm i cluinfinn cuibdius cubaid
>   ac na helaib.

Slúag na faílenn roptís fáiltig
    rér seól súntach
dia rísad Port na Ferg fáiltech
    in Derg Drúchtach.

Rom lín múich i n-ingnais Éirenn
    díamsa coimse;
'sin tír aineóil conam tharla
    taideóir toirse.

Trúag in turus do-breth formsa
    a Rí rúine —
Uch! ní ma-ndechad bu-déine
    do Cath Chúile!

Ba ma-ngénair do macc Dímma
    'na chill chredlaig
airm i cluininn tíar i nDurmaig
    mían dom menmain:

Fúaim na gaíthe frisin leman
    ardon-peitte,
golgaire in luin léith co n-aite
    íar mbéim eitte.

Éistecht co moch i Ros Grencha
    frisin damraid;
coicetal na cúach don fhidbaid
    ar brúach shamraid.

Tréide as dile lem for-ácbas
    ar bith buidnech —
Durmag, Doire, dinn ard ainglech,
    is Tír Luigdech.

> Ro grádaiges íatha Éirenn
> > deilm cen ellach;
> > feis ac Comgall, cúairt co Cainnech,
> > robad mellach.

It would be delightful, Son of Mary, in strange journeys to travel over the sea, the well of floods, to Ireland.

To Mag nÉolairg by Benevanagh across Lough Foyle where I would hear fitting harmony from the swans.

The host of the seagulls would rejoice at our swift sail if the dewy Derg [his ship] were to reach welcoming Port na bhFearg.

Sorrow filled me leaving Ireland when I was powerful, so that mournful grief came to me in the foreign land.

Wretched the journey that was imposed on me, O King of Mysteries — ah, would that I had never gone to the battle of Cúl Dremne!

Lucky for the son of Dímma in his pious cell, where I used to hear westwards in Durrow the delight of my mind:

The sound of the wind playing music to us in the elm-tree, and the cry of the grey blackbird with pleasure when it had clapped its wings.

To listen early in Ros Grencha to the stags, and the cuckoos calling from the woods on the brink of summer.

I have left the three things I love best in the populated world — Durrow, Derry, the high angelic homestead, and Tír Luigdech.

I have loved the lands of Ireland, I speak truth; it would be delightful to spend the night with Comgall and visit Canice.

¶ For the readings of the Brussels MS. see W. Reeves, *Life of St. Columba* (Dublin, 1857), 274; for those of B.IV.2 and 23.N.10, see Kuno Meyer, *ZCP*, VII, 309.

48

LULLABY OF ADVENTUROUS LOVE

The story of the elopement of Díarmait and Grania has come down to us only in a wearisome late-medieval version. This poem is all that remains to us of a twelfth-century version, which was obviously far superior as literature. The four lines on page 112 are all that remains of a still earlier one, and the contrast is striking. The earliest version is the direct naked speech of a woman in a certain situation; this poem bears the same relation to it as a poem of Tennyson's to 'O Western Wind, When Wilt Thou Blow'. Yeats's beautiful 'Lullaby' is an adaptation of it.

It is generally supposed that the description of nature in tumult is intended to describe the hunt for the lovers by her husband, Fionn. More probably it describes a storm.

> Codail beagán beagán beag,
> uair ní heagail duit a bheag,
>   a giolla dá dtardas seirc,
>   a mhic Uí Dhuibhne, a Dhiarmaid.
>
> Codailse sonn go sáimh sáimh,
> a Uí Dhuibhne, a Dhiarmaid áin;
>   do-ghéan-sa t'fhoraire de,
>   a Mheic Uí dhealbhdha Dhuibhne.
>
> Codail beagán, beannacht fort,
> ós uisce Tobráin Tréanghort,

LULLABY OF ADVENTUROUS LOVE

    a uanáin uachtair locha
do bhrú Thíre Tréanshrotha.

Rob ionann is codladh teas
deighFhiodhaigh na n-airdéigeas,
    dá dtug inghin Morainn bhuain
    tar ceann Conaill ón Chraobhruaidh.

Rob ionann is codladh tuaidh
Fionnchaidh Fhionnchaoimh Easa Ruaidh,
    dá dtug Sláinghe, séaghdha rainn,
    tar ceann Fáilbhe Chotatchinn.

Rob ionann is codladh tiar
Áine inghine Gáilían,
    feacht do-luidh céim fo thrilis
    la Dubhthach ó Dhairinis.

Rob ionann is codladh tair
Deadhadh dána dhíomasaigh,
    dá dtug Coinchinn inghin Binn
    tar ceann Deichill déin duibhrinn.

A chró gaile iarthair Ghréag,
anfad-sa dot fhorcoimhéad;
    maidhfidh mo chroidhe-se acht súaill
    monat fhaicear re hénuair.

Ar scaradh ar ndís 'ma-le
scaradh leanabh aonbhaile,
    is scaradh cuirp re hanmain,
    a laoich Locha fionnCharmain.

Léigfidhear caoinche ar do lorg,
rith Caoilte ní budh hanord;
   nachat tair bás ná broghadh,
   nachat léige i sírchodladh.

Ní chodail in damh-sa sair,
ní scuireann do bhúirfeadhaigh;
   cia bheith um dhoiribh na lon
   ní fuil 'na mheanmain codladh.

Ní chodail an eilit mhaol
ag búirfeadhaigh fá breaclaogh;
   do-ní rith tar barraibh tor;
   ní dhéan 'na hadhbhaidh codal.

Ní chodail an chaoinche bhras
ós barraibh na gcrann gcaomhchas;
   is glórach a-táthar ann;
   gi bé an smólach ní chodlann.

Ní chodail an lacha lán;
maith a láthar re deaghshnámh;
   ní dhéan súan ná sáimhe ann,
   ina hadhbhaidh ní chodlann.

A-nocht ní chodail an ghearg
ós fhraochaibh anfaidh iomard;
   binn foghar a gotha glain
   eidir shrotha ní chodail.

Sleep a little, a little little, for you have little to fear, lad I gave love to, Díarmait son of Ó Duibne.

LULLABY OF ADVENTUROUS LOVE

Sleep here, quietly, quietly, grandson of Duibne, noble Díarmait. I shall be your watchman, shapely son of Ó Duibne.

Sleep a little, bless you, over the water of Toprán Trengort. O foam on the lake's surface from the edge of Tír Trénshrotha.

May it be like the southern sleep of great Fidach of the high poets who carried off the daughter of enduring Morann against Conall of the Red Branch.

Let it be like the northern sleep of fair Finnchad of Assaroe when he carried off Slaine, happy choice, from Fáilbe Hardhead.

May it be like the western sleep of Aine, daughter of Gailian, when she eloped into the woods with Dubthach from Dernish.

May it be like the eastern sleep of proud arrogant Dedad when he carried off Coíchenn, daughter of Binn, against stern Deichill Duibrinn.

Fold of valour west of Greece, I shall remain and keep guard; my heart will all but break if at any time I do not see you.

The parting of us two is like the parting of children of one home; it is like the parting of body and soul, hero of fair Loch Carman.

A spell will be laid on your path; Caoilte's race will not be in vain, so that neither death nor grief may come to you, nor lay you in eternal sleep.

This stag eastward does not sleep; he does not cease from bellowing; even though he is in the blackbirds' grove he does not have it in his mind to sleep.

The hornless hind does not sleep, crying for her speckled fawn; she races over the tops of the bushes and does not sleep in her lair.

The flighty linnet does not sleep in the tops of the lovely tangled trees: everything there gives voice, and even the thrush does not sleep.

The heavy duck does not sleep, but plans to swim boldly; she does not rest or linger; in her nest she does not sleep.

The curlew does not sleep tonight over the raging of the wild storm; the sound of his clear voice is sweet; he does not sleep among the streams.

¶ See E. MacNeill, *Duanaire Finn* (London, 1908; ITS, VII), I, 84.

49

A WINTER NIGHT

In this, one of the last flashes of early Irish nature poetry, nothing but the trappings remain; the spirit has fled. As in the 'Lullaby of Adventurous Love' nature is merely a background to the picture of the romantic lover and the old huntsman and fighter.

Since *Agallamh na Seanórach*, the text from which it is taken, was composed at the beginning of the Modern Irish period, we have put it into the appropriate spelling.

> Is fúar geimhreadh, at-racht gaoth;
> éirghidh damh díscir deargbhaoth;
>   ní te a-nocht an sliabh slán
>   gé bheith damh dian ag dordán.
>
> Ní thabhair a thaobh re lár
> damh Shléibhe Cairn na gcomhdhál;
>   ní lugha at-chluin ceol cuaine
>   damh Chinn Eachtgha ionnuaire.
>
> Mise Caoilte, is Diarmaid donn,
> agus Oscar áith éadrom,
>   ro choistmís re ceol cuaine
>   deireadh aidhche adhuaire.
>
> Is maith chodlas an damh donn
> fuil is a chneas re Coronn,

mar do bheith fa Thuinn Tuaighe
deireadh aidhche ionnuaire.

A-niú iosam seanóir sean,
ní aithnim acht beagán fear;
do chroithinn coirrshleigh go cruaidh
i madain oighridh ionnuair.

Ad-lochar do Rígh nimhe,
do mhac Mhuire inghine,
do-bheirinn mór socht ar slúagh
gé bhear an-ocht go hadhuar.

Winter is cold, the wind has risen, the fierce wild stag rises; the virgin mountain is cold tonight though the swift stag is belling.
The stag of Slieve Carn of the assemblies does not lay his side to the ground, and the stag of cold Ceann Eachtgha listens to the music of the wolfpack.
Myself, Caoilte, and brown Diarmaid, and Oscar bright and swift; we listened to the music of the wolfpack at the end of a cold night.
Well sleeps the brown stag who rests his side on Coronn as though he were beneath the wave of Tonn Tuaighe at the end of the cold night.
Today I am old and grave; I recognize few, but I used to brandish a sharp spear bravely in a morning of cold ice.
I thank the King of Heaven, the son of Mary Virgin, often I silenced a host though tonight I am cold.

¶ See W. Stokes' edition of the *Agallamh* (*IT*, IV, 1, 100).

50

MASSACRE OF THE INNOCENTS

This curious poem is from a series of homilies that tell the story of Christ's childhood in the form of a medieval romance; the preacher, like the story-teller, occasionally breaks into dramatized chants, not unlike that which we have given from 'The Only Jealousy of Emer'. The language is late Middle Irish, and we have modernized the spelling.

[A Woman:] Ciodh má ndeilighe mo mhac grádhach
                riom?
   Toradh mo bhronn,
   mé ro thuisimh,
   mo chích ro ibh
   mo bhrú ros iomarchar,
   m'inne ro shúigh,
   mo chridhe ro shás,
   mo bheatha rob é,
   mo bhás a bhreith uaim;
   mo neart ro thráigh,
   m'innsce ro shocht,
   mo shúile ro dhall.

[Another:] Mo mhac bheire uaim,
   ní hé do-ní an t-olc,

               marbh didhiu mé féin,
               ná marbh mo mhac!
               Mo chíocha gan loim,
               mo shúile go fliuch,
               mo lámha ar crith,
               mo chorpán gan níth,
               mo chéile gan mhac,
               mé féine gan neart,
               mo bheatha is fiú bás!
               Uch, m'aonmhac, a Dhé!
               M'fhaoidhe gan luach,
               mo ghalar gan ghein,
               gan díoghail go bráth;
               mo chíocha 'na dtost,
               mo chridhe ro chrom.

[ANOTHER:] Aon shiorthaoi dá mharbhadh,
               sochaidhe mharbhthaoi,
               naoidhin bhuailtí,
               na haithreacha ghontaoi,
               na máithreacha mharbhthaoi,
               ifreann ro líon sibh
               neamh ro dhún sibh,
               fola fírén ro dhoirtseabhar gan chionaidh.

[ANOTHER:] Tair chugam, a Chríost,
               beir m'anmain go luath
               maraon is mo mhac!
               Uch, a Mhuire mhór,
               Máthair Mheic Dé,
               ciodh do-dhéan gan mhac?

> Tríd Mhacsa ro marbhadh
> mo chonn is mo chiall;
> do-rinne bean bhaoth díom
> i ndiaidh mo mheic;
> mo chridhe is caob cró
> a haithle an áir thruaigh
> ó 'ndiu go dtí bráth.

[A WOMAN:] *Why do you part me from my darling son? The fruit of my womb, it was I who bore him, he drank from my breast, my womb carried him, he sucked my bowels, he was my life, it is my death to take him from me. It has sapped my strength, it has stilled my speech, it has blinded my eyes.*

[ANOTHER:] *You take my son from me, it is not he who does the wrong; kill me then, do not kill my son! My breasts without milk, my eyes wet, my hands shaking, my body without mettle, my husband without a son, myself without strength, my life is but death! O God, my only son, my journey [?] without reward, my labour without birth, unrevenged until Doomsday. My breasts are stilled, my heart is bowed down.*

[ANOTHER:] *You seek one to kill, you kill many; you strike down the babies, you wound the fathers, you kill the mothers. You have filled hell, you have shut heaven, you have spilt the blood of the righteous without a cause.*

[ANOTHER:] *Come to me, Christ! Take my life quickly along with my son. O great Mary, Mother of God's Son, what shall I do without a son? On account of your Son my sense and mind have been killed; I have been made a mad woman after my son. My heart is a clot of blood after the tragic slaughter from today till the judgement comes.*

¶ Printed by Kuno Meyer, *GJ*, IV, 88, from the unique MS. LB, fo. 141a.

51

THE LAST CALL-UP

Only an odd word or two differentiates this poem from Modern Irish, and only a certain freshness of approach differentiates it from the conventional religious verse of the four centuries after 1200.

Sluaghadh so re Síol Ádhaimh
is monar ríogh do-rálaigh;
    dá mbeith úaibh nach tigseadh ris
    gá baile a ngeibh a fhorbhais?

Fada a-táthar agá thriall;
raghar, tiaghar, do-chuas riamh;
    beithear agá dhol go bráth
    ó ré aoinfhir go n-anfháth.

Innisfead dóibh, is eol damh,
an leath bhearar an sluaghadh;
    do neoch fo-cheard domhan de
    a mbreith a ndúirtheach n-úire.

Is é do-thaod ar a gceann
athach duaibhseach, dubh a dhreann;
    ad-chí cách, ní fhaiceann neach,
    a Dhé, níorbh ionmhain duibhreach.

Ad-chonnarc a-né gá thriall
óglaoch isa tuaithse tíar;
  dob fhiú a chomhthrom d'ór bhuidhe
  an t-óglaoch fionn foltbhuidhe.

Dá mbeith gá chreic ar gach maigh
gar beag re dtocht an tsluaghaidh,
  dob fhiú céad uinge d'ór cheard
  an fear cródha claidhimhdhearg.

Do bhaoi ballán lán do lionn
isan adhart ós a chionn;
  a-tibh digh ré dtocht ar feacht —
  nochar mhó a íota ar n-imtheacht.

Ionmhain leis a mhacámh buadh,
ionmhain leis a inghean uagh;
  dúthractar uile tocht lais;
  fada leo beith 'na éagmhais.

Ó ro bánaigheadh a bhonn
is ro taithmidheadh a mhong,
  is ro fheac a fheoil re cnáimh,
  ro ba móide leo a mhí-ghráin.

Ó ro sheang a mheadhón mas
is ro shaobh a rosc rionnghlas,
  is ro éirigh a bhruinne,
  do-bhéardaois é ar énuinge.

Résiu ro gabhadh galar
rob fhearr lé mhuintir anadh;

THE LAST CALL-UP

rob fhada leo do bhaoi as-taigh
ó do bhaoi ag triall an tsluaghaidh.

Iongnadh bhearar an sluaghadh
ní do chreich bhó ná bualadh;
   marcaigheacht a ndiaidh a bhonn
   ceathrar agá iomfhulang.

Dá chrann chaola taobh re taobh,
seisean féin ar cleathchor chaol,
   dias 'na dhiaidh, dias roimhe sair,
   seisean gan a n-agallaimh.

A-tá ann iongnadh eile,
nocha bhearar each fa eire,
   nocha bhearar bolg um lón
   leis an sluagh ríoghdha rómhór.

Nocha bhearar ga ná sciath,
nocha bhearar brat ná biadh,
   acht cubhat do léine lín
   um chorpán gach duine díbh.

Robadh maith damhsa, a Mheic Dé,
ar mo rannsa ochaine,
   go bhfaicinnse thiar nó thair
   a bhfuil ag triall an tsluaghaidh.

Cineadh Ádhaimh is Eabha
gona ndaoinibh daithgheala,
   nochan fhuil díbh thiar ná thair
   nach fuil ag triall an tsluaghaidh.

This hosting of Adam's seed, it is a king's labour that summons it. If there be any of you who doesn't want to go, in what house will he stand siege?

People are going a long time on it; they will go, they go, they have gone; they will be going on it for ever since the time of one man of evil purpose.

I'll tell you since I know, where the hosting goes: each one who casts off the world is taken to an earthen barrack.

He who leads them is a gloomy brute with a dark face: he sees everyone and no one sees him; God, the bastard is no pet.

Yesterday I saw a young soldier in the country here to the west who was going on it. That fair, yellow-haired recruit was worth his weight in gold.

If he were being sold at any fair a little before the hosting went, that tough young man with his stout sword would have been worth a hundred ounces of artificer's gold.

He had a basin full of beer on the bedhead over him; he took a drink before he set out; he was not thirsty after his departure.

He liked his fine son, he liked his virgin daughter; they longed to go with him; they worried about being without him.

But when his footsole grew pale, and his hair was cut, and the flesh stuck to his bone, they were filled with horror of him.

When his plump belly caved in, and his keen eye grew dim, and his chest stuck out, they would have given him for an ounce of gold.

Before the illness took him, his family preferred him to stay; when he went on the hosting they longed to get him out of the house.

A marvellous way one goes hosting, not to plunder cattle or cattle yards, but feet first with four of them carrying him.

Two narrow poles side by side, and himself on a wickerwork stretcher; two behind him, two in front, and he not talking to them.

Another marvellous thing is that no one takes a packhorse with him, or brings a knapsack of food on that vast kingly hosting.

No one brings spear or shield; no one clothes or food; nothing but a couple of yards of linen around the body of each man.

O Son of God, for my verse of lament, east or west I should love to see all that are going on the hosting.

The seed of Adam and Eve with all their brightly coloured folk, not one of them, east or west, but is going on the hosting.

¶ Edited by O. Bergin from the unique MS. Book of Lecan, fo. 172a, 49, in the *Irish Review*, II, 248–51.

MEDIEVAL DIARY

As with the earlier period, it is from scraps of poems preserved in metrical and grammatical tracts, or on the margins of manuscripts that we get some of the best of Middle Irish verse. The dates record the deaths of the people referred to.

1. *Murchad's Victory* (994)

A muinter Murchada móir
frisná geib fid ná fíadmóin,
    maidm for barngeintib co Bóinn
    re bar ngallmeirggib gríanshróill.
Sceirdit broid snechta asa sróin
occaib dar Echtga imm íarnóin.

2. *Mael Sechnaill II* (1022)

A choscar derg dédenach
    fescor ocon Áth Buide,
trícha laithe lémennach
    ó shin co cenn a uide.

3. *The Two Queens* (1088)

Mór, ingen meic Thaidg a-túaid
ar-rícht tech d'éccaib díombúaid;
    Dubchoblait oc dul do Chlúain
    i matain fogmair finnfhuair.

4. Conchubhar Ó hAnniaraidh (1096)
> Ní mó grád Gallbraite
> ri Ua Céin Conchobhar
> do chor 'na innarad —
> is é so a fhír —
> indá no díbuirged
> lán glaicce glasubull
> i roimse romessa
> i medón ardchaille
> ó Ríg na ríg.

1. People of great Murrough whom neither wood nor wild moor halts, you have scattered the infidels to the Boyne before your foreign standards of sunbright satin. Snowflakes break from their noses over Slieve Aughty in the late evening.

2. His last red victory was in the evening at Athboy; it was thirty rushing days from that to his journey's end.

3. Mór, the daughter of Tadg's son from the north, has reached the mournful house of the dead, with Dubhchobhlaid going to Clonmacnois on a nippy autumn morning.

4. Conor, king of the Uí Chéin, thinks no more of adding Norse spoils to his incomes — this is the truth — than if a fistful of green apples had been knocked down by the King of Kings in the height of harvest in the middle of a great wood.

¶ 1. *IT*, III, 69, §16. 2. *FM*, anno 1022. 3. *FM*, anno 1088. 4. *IT*, III, 95, §145.

53
MEN AND WOMEN—II

1. *The Poet*

Día nimením thorbai
   imm éicsi n-aird n-amrai;
é fo-cheird cen dolmai
   néim n-óir deirg form labrai.

2. *The Thirsty Poet*

Bendacht úaimm for Eithni n-ollguirm,
   ingen Domnaill dáiles bir,
oca n-esbius íar cúairt chathrach
   for neim nathrach
eire ochtair chethrar bachlach
   síthchenn srathrach, srúaimm di mid.

3. *The Master Builder*

A mo Choimmdiu, cid do-génsa
   frissin adbur mársa?
Cuin bus aicde fo scéim dlútai
   inna deich cét clársa?

4. *Visitors*

Is di bésaib clúanaige,
   áit i fera céilide,

do-tét i tech, saltraid fort
 amal cach mbocc féinnide.

Is é tadall séguinne,
 áit i fera céilide,
do-tét i tech, snaidid crann,
 gaibid rann co éimige.

5. A Girl's Song

Gel cech nua — sásad nglé!
utmall álcha ócduine,
 áilli bretha bíte im sheirc,
 millsi bríathra fir thochmairc.

1. God of Heaven does not disturb me in my high marvellous poetry; he pours freely the beauty of red gold over my utterances.

2. A blessing from me on glorious Eithne, daughter of Domnall who casts a spear, with whom, after searching through a poisonous town, I have drunk a stream of mead that was load enough for thirty-two wry-necked haltered hauliers.

3. O my Lord, what shall I do with all this great material? When shall these thousand planks be a work of art of compact beauty?

4. What the rogue does when he pays a visit is to come into the house and tramp over you like a goatish soldier. What a gentleman does when he pays a visit is to come into the house, to whittle a stick, and to quote an opportune verse.

5. Everything new is neat — cheers! A young man is changeable in his desires, lovely are decisions about love and sweet the words of a man who comes wooing.

¶ 1. *IT*, III, 8, §8. 2. *IT*, III, 72, §28. 3. Laud 610, fo. 10a; printed by Meyer, *Otia Merseiana*, II, 78. 4. LL, fo. 116b, marg. 5. LL, fo. 121a, marg.

54

STORM AND BIRDSONG

The most tantalizing feature of Irish literature is the odd verses that crop up here and there from what must have been whole poems about nature. These in their turn can only have been examples of a literary form that was unique in Europe. They have been ascribed not very convincingly to the hermits of the earlier centuries, and more plausibly by Professor Jackson to pagan rites. The explanation may be simpler than either of these, for we must remember that the Irish professional poets composed in darkness, a practice that certainly ante-dates the use of writing, and nature poetry does not survive the revival of the professional poets — it may almost be said to stop dead at the end of the twelfth century. If we think of the nature poetry as a Christian reaction to a poetry that shut out the light, we may not be far wrong in our guesses as to its origin.

1. *The Sea in Flood*

Fégaid úaib
sair fo-thúaid
in muir múaid
  mílach;
adba rón
rebach rán
ro gab lán
  línad.

2. The Blackbird at Belfast Lough

Int én bec
ro léic feit
do rind guip
   glanbuidi;
fo-ceird faíd
ós Loch Laíg
lon do chraíb
   charrbuidi.

3. The Blackbird

Och, a luin, is buidhe dhuit
   cáit sa mhuine a bhfuil do nead!
A dhíthreabhaigh nách clinn clog
   is binn bog sítheamhail t'fhead.

4. The Blackbird's Song

Int én gaires asin tsail,
   álainn guilbnén as glan gair;
rinn binn buide fir duib druin,
   cas cor cuirther, guth ind luin.

5. The Bee

Daith bech buide a úaim i n-úaim,
   ní súail a uide la gréin;
fó for foluth sa mag már,
   dag a dál, comol 'na chéir.

6. The Great Bog

Úar ind adaig i Móin Móir
feraid dertan ní deróil;

dordán fris tib in gaeth glan
géissid ós caille clithar.

1. See away to the north-west the splendid, whale-haunted sea! The dwelling of seals, sportive and shining, is in full flood.

2. The little bird has whistled from the tip of his bright yellow beak; the blackbird from a bough laden with yellow blossom has tossed a cry over Belfast Lough.

3. Ah, blackbird, it is well for you wherever your nest is in the bush. Hermit who rings no bell, sweet, soft, peaceful is your whistle.

4. The bird that calls from the willow, lovely is his little beak with its pure cry. The sweet yellow bill of the stout black lad; a twisty tune that's played, the blackbird's song.

5. The yellow bee speeds from hollow to hollow, he makes a long journey in the sun, he flies joyously out into the great plain, good is his tryst, the reunion in his hive.

6. Cold is the night in the Great Bog, a terrible rainstorm beats down; a deep song at which the clear wind laughs screams over the shelter of the wood.

¶ 1. *IT*, III, 38, §24. 2. *IT*, III, 99, §167. 3. LB, 36 marg. 4. *IT*, III, 19, §53. 5. See *Bruchstücke*, §159. 6. *IT*, III, 67, §2.

INDEX OF TITLES

Breastplate Number One	27
Breastplate Number Two	33
Colum Cille in Exile	181
Créd's Lament	78
Crucifixion, The	40
Dead Lover, The	86
Downfall of Heathendom, The	61
Dramatis Personae	107
Eve	157
Ex-Poet, The	75
Faith	161
Fellow Feeling	154
Four Seasons, The	140
Grace before Death	171
Hermitage, The	148
Hymn to St. Colum Cille	19
Hymn to St. Michael	165
Invocation to the Martyrs	56
Ita and the Infant Jesus	102
Jesus and the Sparrows	23
Jesus at School	25
Lament for Fer Diad, The	174
Last Call-up, The	195
Líadan	72
Lullaby of Adventurous Love	184
Mael Ísu finds his Psalter again	167
Massacre of the Innocents	191
Medieval Diary	200
Men and Women — I	111
Men and Women — II	202
Nativity, The	36

Nun of Beare, The	48
Only Jealousy of Emer, The	130
Ordeal by Cohabitation	77
Paradise Revised	115
Pilgrim, The	151
Pity of Nature — I, The	100
Pity of Nature — II, The	179
Prayer for a Long Life	123
Prayer for Recollection, A	144
Rónán's Lament	93
St. Brigit, To	67
Scholar and his Cat, The	81
Scribe, The	159
Song of the Heads, The	176
Storm and Birdsong	205
Summer	137
Tempest, The	126
Triads	104
Two Worlds, The	44
Winter	98
Winter	134
Winter Night, A	189
Writing Out-of-doors	84

INDEX OF NAMES

Ádam (Adam), 115 ff., 157, 195
Aed Bennán, 107
Aed Connacht, 109
Aed mac Ainmire, 7
Aed mac Colggan, 107
Aed mac Sétnai, 63
Agallamh na Seanórach, 189
Aidne, 79
Ailill, 86
Ailill Áne, 68
Áine, 185
Alba (Scotland), 128
Alenn, 11, 62, 68
Annae (Annas), 41
Ard Machae (Armagh), 61
Armagh, 6, 14
Ascoli, G. I., 27
Áth Buide, 200
Áth Rois, 134

Balagh Moon, 151, 176
Banna, 179
Bar Abbán (Barabbas), 42
Beann Fhoibne, 181
Beanna Bó, 135
Bécc mac Éogain, 63
Bede, 5
Beithel (Bethlehem), 37, 38
Berbae, 64
Bergin, Osborn, 84, 199
Binchy, D. A., 33
Bláthmacc, 11, 36, 40, 44
Bóinn, 200
Bran mac Febail, 44, 45

Bregon, 50
Bresal mac Déin, 69
'Bricriu's Feast' (*Fled Bricrenn*), 12, 130
Bridges, Robert, 12
Brigit (St. Bridget), 62, 67 ff.

Cainnech (saint), 183
Caiphas, 41
Cairbre Nia Fer, 69
Calad Nit, 127
Caoilte, 186, 189
Carney, James, 4, 16, 23, 24, 36, 39, 60, 161, 164, 167, 170, 171
'Cattle Raid of Cooley' (*Táin Bó Cúalgne*), 6, 174
Cearbhall, 176
Cellach (saint), 8
Cend Tíre, 128
Charlemagne, 12
Cíarán (saint), 62, 64
Clárach, 87
Clonfert, 8, 72, 75
Clonmacnois (*Clúan moccu Nois*), 6, 11, 12, 14, 200
Clúan moccu Nois, 62
Coill Ché, 135
Coill Chuan, 14, 135, 138
Coinchenn, 185
Colmán (saint), 79
Colmán mac Léníni, 3, 4
Colum Cille, 2, 16, 19, 20, 159, 181
Comgall (saint), 183

INDEX OF NAMES

Conaing, 108
Conall, 185
Conchobar Ó hAnniaraidh, 201
Connachta, 108, 109
Corann, 189
Corc, 69
Cormac mac Cuileannáin, 16, 151, 176
Créd, 7, 8, 78
Crimthann, 68
Crínóc, 167
Cronán (saint), 64
Cú Chulainn, 6, 7, 130, 174
Cuirithir, 7, 8, 72 ff.
Cúl Dremne, 19, 181, 182
Cummíne (saint), 7, 8, 9, 72 ff.
Currech, 68

Daithlenn, 94
Dallán Forgaill, 2
Deichell, 185
'Destruction of Dá Derga's Hostel' (*Togail Bruidne Dá Derga*), 6
Díarmait (king), 115
Díarmait Ó Duibhne, 16, 184
Dillon, Myles, 27, 133
Dínertach, 7, 78
Dobarchú, 75
Doíléne, 94
Doire, 179
Domnall, 3
Donn, 90
Donnchad, 64
Druim Daill, 14, 138
Dubchoblait, 200
Dubhthach, 185
Dún nÁis, 94
Dún Sebairche, 94
Durmag, 182

Eba, Eua, Eabha (Eve), 115 ff., 157, 197
Echaid, 93
Echtge, Eachtgha, 189
Égept (Egypt), 37
Eithne, 202
Emain Machae, 62
Emer, 6, 130 ff., 191
Éoganacht, 107
Étaín, 6
Etan, 111

Fáilbe Cotatchenn, 185
Fand, 130
Féic, 86
Feidilmid, 108
Femen, 50
Fer Diad, 7, 174
Ferna, 63
Finn, 184
Finnbarr (saint), 16
Fionnchadh, 185
Fothad Canainne, 86 ff.

Géagán, 176
Glendalough (Glenn Dá Locha), 7, 62
Glenn Ridhe, 135
Gormfhlaith, 176
Gort, 78
Grania (Gráinne), 16, 112, 184
Gúaire, 7, 8, 9, 78

Herúaid (Herod), 36 ff.
Hopkins, Gerard Manly, 126
Horace, 12, 26

Í (Iona), 20
Ierosalem (Jerusalem), 36

INDEX OF NAMES 213

Inber na Dá Ainmech, 127
Inis Fáil, 134
Inis Scit, 127
Iona, 19
Iosiab (Joseph), 23
Ita (saint), 102

Jackson, K. H., 13, 205
John (saint), 16
Jordan, 115

Kildare, 11, 12
Kipling, Rudyard, 56

Laserian (saint,) 33
Leinster, 67
Leitir Cró, 135
Leitir Dá mBruach, 86
Ler, 126
Líadan, 7, 8, 72 ff.
Life, 67
Lismore, 165
Loch Carman, 185
Loch Dá Dam, 107
Loch Febail, 181
Loeg, 130
Loegaire, 61, 68
Lorc, 69
Lothlind, 113
Lugaid, 63
Luicifer, 115 ff.

Mac Dá Cerda, 7
MacNeill, E., 188
Mael Fhothartaig, 93 ff.
Mael Ísu Ó Brolchán, 16, 72, 165, 167, 171
Mael Rúain, 64
Mael Sechnaill, 200

Mag nÉolairg, 181
Mag Luirg, 134
Mag Mell, 44, 45
Mag Mon, 44
Mag Rath, 100, 179
Maire (Mary), 36, 52; Mairenat, 37
Manannán mac Lir, 45, 127
Manchán (saint), 148
Mangan, James Clarence, 17
Meyer, Kuno, 17, 33, 35, 48, 71, 76, 80, 92, 93, 97, 106, 129, 136, 139, 144, 147, 150, 151, 153, 156, 158, 160, 166, 167, 170, 173, 183, 194
Míchél (Michael), 118, 165
Mide, 64, 108
Mo Chumma, 19, 20
Mo Laise, 16
Mongán, 7
Mór, 200
Morann, 185
Morrígan, 89
Murchad, 200
Murphy, Gerard, 13, 14, 48, 55, 148, 160

Níall Glúndub, 176
Níall Noígíallach, 20, 167
Nun of Beare, 7, 8, 9, 48 ff.

O'Daly, M., 125
Oengus of Clonenagh, 10, 36, 56, 67
O'Keeffe, J. G., 180
Orthanach, 11, 67
Oscar, 189

Pangur, 12, 81
Patrick, Pátraic (saint), 16, 27, 61, 181

Phaedra, 93
Piláit (Pilate), 41

Reeves, W., 183
Róim (Rome), 112
Rónán (king), 7, 93 ff.
Rónán (saint), 7
Ros Grencha, 182
Rumann, 126

Sacharias, 25
Saltair na Rann, 115 ff.
Saxain, 127
Scuithín (saint), 16
Sedulius, 12, 81
Seymour, St. John D., 122
'Sick-bed of Cú Chulainn' (*Serglige Con Culainn*), 12
Sláinghe, 185
Sliabh Cairn, 189
Stokes, W., 122, 190

Suibne Geilt, 7, 100, 179
Swords, 11

Tara (Temair), 67
Temair, 61
Thurneysen, R., 3
Tobrán Tréanghort, 184
Tonn Tuaighe, 190
Tortiu, 108
Túaim Inbir, 100
Tulach na Ríogh, 177

Uí Néill, 67, 78

Van Hamel, A. G., 47
'Vision of Mac Con Glinne', 6

'Wooing of Emer', 6
'Wooing of Étaín', 6

Yeats, W. B., 16, 184